MW00939989

INTERVENTION
Your True Identity

VONJOHN

XULON PRESS

Xulon Press
2301 Lucien Way #415
Maitland, FL 32751
407.339.4217
www.xulonpress.com

Printed in the United States of America.

Paperback ISBN-13: 978-1-6312-9399-3

Intervention

B efore they entered the room, she had a sense of what needed to be said. After all the introductions were made and the formalities were done, she had decided, in her mind, to share her knowledge, as well as receive what the counselor had to offer. Besides, Delanie and her husband, Douglas, **were** the ones seeking help.

Dr. Sarai Fulton, B.S, M.S, MSW, PH.D., who was in her mid-forties, had a long list of accolades in the field of academics. She had degrees in science, medicine, social work, and psychology. Her and her husband were married for ten years with no children of their own. They had separate practices. They would feed off of one another's experiences concerning their perspective clients without breaking any confidentiality clauses. Little did they know by taking on Delanie and Douglas Revel as clients of the level of deception that would be exposed in their own marriage.

Delanie began with, "I have to admit I have reservations about coming here today. I'll be honest, and I hope it doesn't offend anyone. But, this puts me in a very compromising position, Dr. Fulton. May I call you Dr. Sarai?"

Dr. Fulton replied, "I prefer Dr. Fulton."

Delanie was just trying to test her and feel her vibes. Delanie wanted to see how Dr. Fulton would respond. Delanie was very successful in provoking people in order to do her own analysis.

Had the doctor said yes to her calling her "Dr. Sarai," she would then believe the doctor was the "easy-going" type and willing to have a transparent doctor/client relationship. Since she didn't, Delanie believed the doctor was anal. This determined how much Delanie would be willing to openly share. Delanie decided not to say what she was going to say after all.

Her thoughts superseded logic, and her beliefs were that counselors, doctors, shrinks, or psychologists were educated fools who had received so many degrees that they themselves were the ones detached from reality. Also, since they spent so much time in books written by mere humans, where would they have time to read or study the most important book of all?.. the Bible. Not to imagine how these scholars were so infiltrated with other people's "junk," messy choices, and ideas that they themselves tended to be burned out or less effective in truly helping anyone. These accredited individuals were taught to believe they had the skills and mindsets to heal others when, in fact, it is actually God who is the Healer, The Great Physician. He's given us the Holy Spirit who is the real counselor.

She would keep this to herself for now.

Instead, Delanie said, "Dr. Fulton? I feel I'm being put in a compromising position when it comes to talking about my husband. I believe in God. I read the Bible and it guides my decisions. I want to be careful not to uncover my house by speaking on certain areas of me and my husband's lives," she said. *Especially with someone who requested we stay formal*, she thought to herself. "Not to mention, Dr. Fulton, some people absolutely cannot handle the truth," said Delanie.

Mark 6:35, 1 Timothy 3:12, Proverbs 14:1, Proverbs 31:10-31

"They say the truth will set you free. And the truth is, it has made some men flee. Then the woman will be 'free,' *all right*. And the man will be free to be with another woman or another man."

Delanie looked at her husband, Douglas. She wanted to read his expression but couldn't quite interpret it. Delanie continued, "The Scriptures," she hesitated, "the ones in the Bible, were written years ago when the regard for women was that of dominance. Women were influential throughout the Bible but with a high submissive undercurrent. If you look really closely, the women of the Bible resemble the women of today. That's why you have to study the Word—right, Doug?"

He had a reply, but his wife didn't skip a beat in her opinionated comments. Although she sometimes revealed truths and Douglas truly loved Delanie, he really needed to set some boundaries.

Dr. Fulton spoke up. "Mrs. Revel, would you mind allowing your husband to comment?"

"I would like to finish making my point before I forget what I'm saying, if you don't mind. It is easy to get off the subject and lose your train of thought," Delanie said. "I want to communicate this so you can understand the point I'm making with the perspective I'm intending to reveal it. Thank you! Now, where was I? Oh, women are to honor their husbands and not bring any harm to them, to love and cherish them. But, there is a time and season for everything. Seasons can shift quickly." Delanie went on, "I need to be clear whether this is the appropriate time to expose flaws in our marriage or not. This can go smoothly with God at the helm of the boat, or shall I say, ship. God is always in control. Would you agree? But, we cause God to have to be creative when getting us to listen to Him and walk in obedience. I want to say a lot of things, but I need to have a sense of peace about not allowing my words or actions to cause additional problems in my life or in my husband's life. I want God to govern our marriage and… our decisions. Do you believe in God, Dr. Fulton?" Delanie knew she didn't.

Dr. Fulton took a very deep breath. "I believe you and Mr. Revel agreed to seek my services for one hour a week to start. I do not want to spend your time focused on me and my religious beliefs. I would like to hear more about you both and hear what thoughts Mr. Revel would like to share. Interestingly enough, we are almost out of time. Would you like to share something else today in the remaining ten minutes we have, Mrs. Revel? Would you like to say anything, Mr. Revel?"

Douglas looked in Dr. Fulton's direction. He had the intention of speaking. It showed in his eyes. Then came a comment from Delanie.

"Yes, Dr. Fulton, I would," she said. "It is important that you notate our sessions. I don't see a pen or pad. Do you have a hidden camera? Do you record our sessions on some modern device? Is there a way we can have a copy on disc of our conversations? Do you have an iPad or some way to email your daily analysis, questions, or comments or even questions we should ask ourselves as part of this therapy?"

If Dr. Fulton believed in God or Jesus, this would be a good time to call on Him *now!* Dr. Fulton took another deep breath and said " Yes" to all of Delanie Revel's questions.

When Mr. and Mrs. Revel left Dr. Fulton's practice, they looked at one another, smiled, and kissed each other deeply, then headed toward their parked car.

Dr. Fulton sipped on her third cup of decaffeinated coffee and tried to remember why she went to college all those years to get into this field. Any field, career, or job that involves people and their journeys in life is exhausting, depleting, exhilarating, and, ultimately, rewarding. All interactions with mankind are learning and testing experiences, she reminded herself.

Dr. Fulton would normally call her husband after one of these sessions. Her husband's practice was really growing. There was a chance she wouldn't be able to reach him. She called him anyway and reached his secretary.

"Thank you for calling Fulton Therapeutics Family Practice, Zoe speaking."

"Hi, Zoe, is Dr. Fulton available? This is important, Zoe. I really need to speak to that wonderful hunk of a man that I married," said Dr. Fulton.

Zoe smiled. She recognized Sarai's voice. "Hi, Mrs. Fulton. How are you? Yes, I believe he is available. Let me connect you."

"Dr. Fulton on the line," he said in humor.

"Honey?" she said. "I just wanted to hear your voice." Sarai felt depleted after her last patients' appointment. "Could we do something relaxing tonight?"

Sarai knew how important it is to keep balance in your marriage and in life. She knew how much Adam and her meant to one another. They were awesome together. She loved her husband so much. She knew how much he loved her, also.

"I was thinking the very same thing," he said. "We could meet at our favorite place.

There's a jazz band playing tonight at 8:00. Think you could be there by 6:00 pm?"

"I could be there *now* sipping on a glass of wine—on second thought, drinking a strong shot of vodka after my last appointment," she said.

"That bad?" Adam laughed.

Sarai smiled. "I'll look forward to you just holding me, honey. That's what I really need—to be in the arms of my loving, sweet, handsome husband."

Adam felt a rush. He loved when his wife affirmed him. He followed up with, "I look forward to holding my lady, too. Is it my turn to rub every inch of your body, massaging some hot oil in places…?" Adam had to turn his attention back to his practice. His secretary had just buzzed in on the intercom reminding him of his next appointment.

Sarai overheard and said, "I love you, honey. I know you have to get back to work."

He said, "Yes, baby. I'll see you in a few hours. Don't be late. Love you."

I'm not ready to tell my story, Delanie thought to herself. She knew that part of this journey called life required her to die to what she wants, die to her fleshly desires and emotions, and die to the need to always be comfortable versus being at peace—the peace and rest that only comes from God.

Anyone who believes that this world can offer peace and happiness is out of their minds. Also, they're living in a fantasy mindset. Even in fantasies, there can be trouble, problems, and death. In some fantasies, in order for the hero/heroine to have victory, the villain has to die. It represents the age-old battle between good and evil. The struggle and victory get recorded continuously in a book, a biography, a letter, a testimony—even in the Bible. The Scriptures are compiled with stories of Jesus, people testifying of experiences and events that took place in their lives and the lives of others.

That which has been is what will be, That which is done is what will be done, and there is nothing new under the sun.
Eccl 1:9 NKJV

The scripture means history repeats itself. The experiences of the past affect current modern-day culture. We are still fighting the relentless battle of sin. Everything God created is relative. We still need one another to survive despite the myths of this iGeneration, with our iPhones, iPads, ISIS wars, Illuminati mindsets, selfies, and "I did it on my own" mentality. No one has done anything on their own. God, through someone or something, helped. If you look at the doctors who believe they give life, then look at if God had not put breath in their lungs, they would not be alive to do anything. Look at a garden that is planted. It needs sun and rain. Look at the soil that is needed (which neither you or I created) for the plants to grow. Even the insects and the animal poop play some part in the scheme of things. An entrepreneur does not build his/her business alone. It takes a lot of information that people compile to bring a successful outcome, feeding off one another's energy. Let's not forget the time, energy, and special moments individuals sacrifice away from family and loved ones to help perfect strangers out of some pretty bad situations. What about the behind-the-scene supporters (specifically God the Father, God the Son, God the Holy Spirit—the Helper) who are barely recognized for their vision, talents, and abilities? Sadly, the activity of humans during their lifetimes will be lost in the scheme of things and will soon be forgotten.

The thief cometh not, but for to steal and kill and to destroy. I am come that they may have life, and that they may have it more abundantly. John 10:10 NKJV

But, there is something new by way of God the Son, Jesus Christ.

Delanie would strongly urge people not to say, "Nobody ever did anything for me." It's a lie that most people believe and impose on others to believe. "Refrain from making it a habit to speak curses on yourself," Delanie would say. It would not be surprising if they got fifty feet away and said it again. It's a huge mystery of how it's easier to remember the bad experiences versus the good ones. Perhaps, it's because adversity teaches us valuable lessons. Painful times often have the most impact. They are the most notable even in the news.

Of course, Delanie had her share of painful times. Each one had brought her to a new level in maturity. Each dark experience brought her closer to God. Each hardship produced humility and character, and each test she passed brought her divine knowledge (aka wisdom that came from God). Oh, but, those were just some of the gifts. She could now move more freely in who she was created to be. Then, when the time was right, she, just like so many of God's creations, would get to teach and reach others to tell the story of His goodness and His glory, ultimately bringing those chosen to greater faith in God. The power and strength in us increases.

How could anyone but, God know the truth about her past? If she began to let her therapist, Dr. Fulton, in on some of the seasons of her life, what evaluation or assessment would the educated doctor come up with? Delanie truly did not need another illness, condition, or misdiagnosis spoken over her or handed to her with a prescription bottle. Unless, God spoke through Dr. Fulton, Delanie did not want to hear it. Chances of that happening would be next to none because Dr. Sarai Fulton did not have a relationship with nor a belief in God, let alone Jesus. However, she could still be used by God. God's abilities are limitless. Mankind's boundaries are limited. God is the God of impossibilities. Let's never forget this truth.

Delanie refused to welcome another conversation with someone who believed in the "universe." Wisdom allows us to know that you cannot worship the creation without at least acknowledging the Creator. The truth is, God created mankind with the gifts, talents, abilities, and even the vision, who, in turn, create the product or thing. Keeping that perspective would and should reveal why we must not only believe in but worship God, not the universe. We recognize there are those who worship their car, even their technological devices. Great example, e.g. the cell phone, the TV. Each of these items has a brand on them letting you know who produced or distributes them. The company will be on the label and/or in the instruction manual. When there is a defect, do we go to the item itself? We go to customer service and/or the customer service of the company who designed it. We use the support of the service to get the defect or malfunction resolved. It's the same concept as when we go to God with any and everything. We come with an instruction manual as well. It's called the Bible. It's funny how most of us refrain from reading the Bible when it's so crucial to our existence. Use discernment and let us go deeper and take our cares, concerns, and problems to God, bypassing humans, and watch His handling of it all—His supernatural power at its best, His Glory, His Way.

Yes, if you cry out for discernment and lift up your voice for understanding, if you see her as silver and search for her as for hidden treasure, then you will understand the Fear of the Lord, and find the knowledge of God. Proverbs 2:3-5 NKJV

That's exactly what Delanie and her husband Doug had witnessed. Did they really need Dr. Fulton? Or did Dr. Fulton need them? Absolutely yes to both questions. God is big on relationships. We just need to make sure our relationship with Him is first.

God is big on marriage. Marriage is created by God and is the primary most sacred relationship on earth. Marriage is profound. It will cause you to look more to Jesus. It will cause you to look more like Jesus and obtain His character. When you endure in marriage, grow, and be willing to change, you will develop the ability to truly love, have a peace (that you won't understand), obtain joy (not to be confused with the myth happiness), be kind, be good, be gentle, have patience (which is produced by suffering long), obtain self-control, and become faithful. These are the fruits of the Spirit, God's Spirit.

Galatians 5:22

Marriage is the one relationship that God approved as the vessel, first and foremost, designed to create other humans (they start out as children). They are to be raised under the teaching of God's instruction and principles. We really got away from the original plan.

Relationships are important, too. Mankind is a result of relationships. Most relationships reflect humans doing it their way, not God's. We need healthy ones and unhealthy ones to grow.

Some relationships will make or break you. Relationships have built and destroyed countries, even kingdoms. The reason Jesus, the Son, came in human form to earth was to restore the relationship (the one that was destroyed because of disobedience and sin) to our God, the Father. There was a separation between God and His creation.

Another reason Jesus came in human form was to save our souls. He came to teach us how to be in healthy relationships within ourselves, with Him, and with one another.

You have to love the relationship between God the Father, God the Son, and God the Holy Spirit—the Trinity. They are so unified, working together so beautifully.

Dr. Sarai Fulton and her husband, Adam, had no idea what that very unified Trinity had in store for them. By any means necessary, they would come to know the Truth.

Delanie and Douglas met six years prior to getting married. Delanie initially did not like him when they were introduced at a night club, by mutual friends, on a double date. It was Cecelia, her best friend, who had introduced them. Cecelia was in an abusive relationship with her boyfriend, Zaen (it's pronounced Zane). His name should've been Insane Whozane. The young man had major personality defects—yes, another angry-spirited male who needed someone to perform an exorcism on him. He started to behave really badly after he and Cecelia were together a few years. Initially, he had been controlled, and no one had been able to see his evil nature and character flaws. Besides, they all were very young. However, if Delanie would have believed that Douglas was anything like his friend, she wouldn't have let him pursue her.

Douglas and Zaen were pseudo-friends. There are times when the cliché "birds of a feather flock together" does not apply. Douglas and Zaen were different. Zaen worked factory setting-type jobs while badgering Cecelia when no one was looking, while Douglas was wearing the badge of bad, defiant college-boy, trying to fit into Zaen's world.

The one thing that Delanie and Cecelia saw that the guys had in common was a huge appetite for sex—horny. Horny is the slang that defines lust-filled individuals. *Just think—yes, "horny" is what Satan's depiction is, pitchfork and all.* It's one of Satan's characteristics and a trap he uses to distract someone from being godlike.

The other thing that the guys had in common was they liked to drink beer. Not just any beer—Colt 45. A famous actor would say in the commercial ad, "Don't let the smooth taste fool ya." Delanie would say, "Colt 45 will make a fool outta you." After years of drinking it, Douglas switched to a beer that was sold in other neighborhoods because he listened to Delanie. Colt 45, Old English, Coke 900 were sold in the impoverished, minority, and ghetto areas. These beers' side effects are anger.

Fast forward—Douglas is now an educator who teaches the youth about this trap to destroy the minds and bodies of young men and women.

He also taught me and said to me. Let your heart retain My words. Keep My commandments and live. Get wisdom! Get understanding! Do not forget nor turn away from the words of My mouth. Do not forsake her and she will preserve you. Love her, and she will keep you. Proverbs 4:4-6 NKJV

Douglas really pursued Delanie. Mostly because she was not attracted to him at all.

Delanie hated the taste and smell of beer. When they were all together, Zaen, Cecelia, and Douglas drank beer. She smoked cigarettes so her breath was probably no better.

Douglas was trying to impress her, so he decided to drink mixed drinks or Courvoisier as time went on. He loved her from the beginning.

Douglas was very intelligent but had mischievous veins in his body. He decided on their tenth date to kidnap Delanie. She was not a virgin but had been with only one other guy in her young life. She was not planning to have sex with anyone other than that young man and had plans to be his wife one day.

Douglas called her pager, impromptu. He arranged to pick her up. She didn't have a car. Douglas had a very clean, pale, yellow convertible with white leather seats. *Impressive*, she thought when he got there. She had never had a guy with a car pick her up before. He didn't tell her where they were going. They headed out of the city. She didn't notice that until they were crossing the Wyn Whithall Bridge. She began to get nervous. There were no cell phones back then. She couldn't exactly jump out of the car. She wouldn't be able to catch a public bus or even a train in this area. She decided not to panic. He handed her a wine cooler at this point. They drove for about an hour toward Trenton, New Jersey. That's where he planned his seduction.

They pulled up to a hideaway cove. It had five wood slated houses around a small lake. The houses were in a cul-de-sac type of alignment. Each house's driveway led to the water, making it beachfront style property. It was so quiet, so beautiful. Delanie's guards were down now. They got out of the car and went to sit on the beach of the lake. They talked, then walked.

The six pack of wine coolers were now gone. Douglas led her to believe they were headed back to the city. Not Mr. Seducer. He told her his mother owned the property behind them. Delanie looked where he was pointing. It was the most quaint house she'd ever seen. It had a woman's touch. Hanging flowers and flowers in planters were everywhere. He got the key from out of one of the planters. They went inside. It had a log cabin feel in most areas of the house. The kitchen was renovated with an island counter in the center.

He poured a little stronger drink for himself and gave Delanie a glass of wine. The refrigerator held pre-seasoned T-bone steaks and enough food to last for days. He started preparing dinner for them. Little did she know this would be their home for the weekend.

After the great dinner, good conversation, and smooth touches, they explored each other in intimacy. Because of Douglas's father-given equipment, Delanie had doubts whether she actually had ever been intimate prior to Doug. Sure didn't feel like she had. She was sore for days. She no longer had plans to marry the other guy now that she had consummated with Doug. She felt guilty. Doug knew he wanted to be with Delanie for the rest of his life.

This was not the vision Doug's mother and sister, Paula and Paula, Jr., had for their precious *"living on a pedestal"* son and brother. They deemed Delanie as the "little fast one" who didn't have enough value to be with college-bound, successful Douglas.

Delanie didn't see this curve coming. After their interlude weekend, Delanie could not see to what extent Doug was willing to risk to be with her. She was sure that somewhere in the law, what happened that weekend, could be looked upon as a kidnapping, almost sexual co-ercion. Except she couldn't prove that she had told him to take her home prior to telling him she couldn't have sex with him. He had finally convinced her, after many failed attempts, that he wanted to make love to her. She stopped speaking to Doug for months afterwards. This was possible because there were no cell phones, Twitter, Facebook, etc.

at that time. He didn't have her home telephone number, either. Zaen and Cecelia orchestrated their next meetings.

Delanie, deep down, wanted the first guy, her first, to love her like Doug did. Trey, Delanie's first, was busy sleeping with his female military "friends" from other cultures. He was internationally making babies without even leaving the country.

Over the next six years, Delanie would be challenged with her emotions for Trey.

Doug would be challenged with his female relatives who believed he was "too good for Delanie (his future wife). They never knew about the weekend by the lake. They never knew about her carrying his child. A child that would never live life on this earth. Judgment without the entire story always leads to destruction.

Wonder what diagnosis the "good ole' doctor" would have for this behavior? Delanie believed Dr. Fulton probably thought she was the trouble in the marriage—the controlling one.

Doug and Delanie eventually started seeing one another. It was inevitable on many accounts. They had friends in common. And despite the age-old occurrence, when others (especially family) think they know who's better for whom, God had a plan.

For My thoughts are not your thoughts, nor are your ways My ways, says the Lord. For as the heavens are higher than the earth, so are My Ways higher than your ways. And My thoughts than your thoughts. Isaiah 55:8-9 NKJV

Doug began to drink more heavily because of the weight of conflict within himself and with his family. His lack of self-control even put a wedge in the close friendship between Delanie and Cecelia. He mischievously joked around and told Zaen that Delanie had told him about Zaen's and Cecelia's love life. It was a joke, but Doug could tell a lie without any facial expression to give it away. One would never know he was not serious.

Zaen (a human time bomb), the last person you would want to trigger, blew up, beat Cecelia, and mandated Cecelia never associate with Delanie again. Even though Doug admitted he was only playing, the friendship was dissolved.

Eventually, Delanie forgave Doug. His grades in his college courses were affected by all of this which had his family convinced it was Delanie's fault. "He should leave that girl alone," said the Paulas. And he did. The family must come first is what had been ingrained in Doug.

They were not aware of the time when he lived in a filthy house that was under construction with no water, electricity, or heat. Delanie had stuck by him. She had given him money and fed him for a season during those struggling college years and over countless nights, helped him study when she had to go to work in the morning.

Now Delanie had lost her first love, her best friend, and Doug. She also lost their baby she was carrying. A child that would never experience life on this earth. Delanie never disclosed this to anyone.

Sin may look good or feel good, but it always leads to destruction.

For the wages of sin is death...But the gift of God is eternal life through Jesus Christ, Our Lord. Romans 6:23 KJV

That scar tissue was thick. It took years of prayer and repentance to heal from that one. One of Delanie's daily prayers was that people, especially females globally, be kind and supportive of one another. The enemy has used males for centuries to hurt us deeply.

You never know what a "sister" (of any culture) is actually dealing with.

After Doug's college graduation and his four failed relationships, he looked Delanie up. They met at the mall for months and after many 2-3 hour conversations over a year span, they reunited. Doug had a way of getting what he wants. God has a way of making us want what He wills — His way.

They were married in June of 2000. They had three children — twin males, aged twenty, who were conceived before their marriage, and a nine-year-old daughter. The twins were a result of an affair Doug had when the family had chosen a "more qualified" woman for Doug. She was subsequently found dead in her car in the mountains in Colorado. She was driving the Jaguar that Doug had bought her.

The car you choose usually says something about your character. The car someone (i.e. your parents) buys for you, does not. It will probably be what they can afford or feel it is safe for you to drive. *And that's exactly what will happen with the twins when the time is right*, thought Delanie.

The twins were only three when their mother died mysteriously. They made the most handsome ring-bearers at Doug's and Delanie's wedding. They were brave little boys considering that they had lost their mother a little over a year prior.

Doug never loved Nina, their biological mother. The Paulas wanted him to get away from Delanie and did everything in their power to make it happen. Look at what others outside a true love relationship can do. Words hold power. They would speak so lowly of Delanie because it appeared she was not the one for Douglas.

Nina was very attractive. She came from a six-figure household, and her future looked promising. Both her parents were what the Paulas would consider a healthy family because they lived in the suburbs. Nina had never told anyone other than Doug that her father had an insatiable appetite for sex with her. Her mother would allow her father to sleep with other teenage girls, from time to time, just so he wouldn't leave her or sleep with his own daughter.

Nina shared with Doug that she did not want to marry for that very reason. She failed to mention that she was in love with someone else.

Nina had completed her freshman year studying to be an engineer when she was told she would be giving birth to twins in four months. She had health problems where she would have irregular menstrual cycles. She also would have migraine headaches where she would take anything she could get her hands on to stop the pain. This very thing irregulated her body. She had no idea that her own father had brought this on. Deep inside, she was stressed by his behavior with these young girls. She watched how her mother, who was lively, kind, and loving, had become bitter, withdrawn, and cold. This man set the cycle for dysfunction or, biblically put, generational curses in motion at a rapid speed. He invited the devil in his house, in their souls, in his children's lives, and his children children's lives. Oh, but it doesn't stop there. Anyone who was connected to them directly or indirectly would be affected. Things like this affect us all.

If My people who are called by My name will humble themselves and pray and seek My face and turn from their wicked ways, then I will hear from heaven and will forgive their sin and heal their land. 2 Chronicles 7:14 NKJV

It is so pathetic how the lust of the eye tears down nations. And to think there are those who are adamantly intentional about finding a beautiful man or woman only to strip them of their outer beauty with tattoos, poisonous perfumes, excessive make-up, domestic violence, body alterations or strip them of their inner beauty with controlling habits, drugs (prescribed and street), excessive sex, insults, rejection, lack of affection, and lack of love. God is love, people! We are nothing, can do nothing, can't fulfill anything without the love of God. When filled with God's Spirit and love, nothing that Satan—the devil, the enemy—or his minions can deceptively throw our way will penetrate or destroy us.

No weapon formed against you shall prosper. And every tongue which rises against you in judgment, you shall condemn. This is The heritage of the servants of the Lord and their righteousness is from Me, says the Lord. Isaiah 54:17 NKJV

Nina's father got delivered after Nina died. The death of someone or something brings forth new life. The consequences are inevitable, but there will be new beginnings.

The consequences of his sins were immediate. He had prostate cancer, which led to other complications. The twins had to help him regularly, along with paid nursing care.

His wife, Nina's mother, gave her life to Christ and left him. She was working with the top organization against sex-trafficking, the A-21 campaign. She committed her life to these victims, causing her to travel around the world. Her rescues wondered why she cried so often night and day. She might not be a good candidate for false eyelashes but, she was a great choice for this assignment as long as her focus stays on God.

All throughout the Bible, God used the least likely to accomplish His purposes.

Jesus's willingness to be bound by man, willingness to die for our sins, and willingness to love us unconditionally is stellar and applicable to so many. This family was forgiven, no matter how ugly the sin. No matter how deep the darkness, no matter how long it takes, the Light of the world (Jesus) will come and have victory. People will face the consequences. But they will help so many others despite their weaknesses, flaws, and hor-rific choices.

Nina had a large insurance policy on her life, which would pay a significant amount of money to the twins when they came of age. Did I say significant? A very significant amount of money. Her death was not ruled as a homicide because she had a history of medical complications. The coroners findings and results suggested she may have had an aneurysm. Since her body was found six months after her death, the decompo-sition made it hard to be exact. Doug's mother and sister (the Paulas) had been helping him care for the twins since they were born. Nina may have looked like what they wanted as a daugh-ter-in-law/sister-in-law but not for long. Nina secretly hated the way they were always trying to control her and Doug's rela-tionship. They were making plans to get married on numerous occasions, but for one reason or another, it never happened.

Nina's sorority sisters were going up to a lodge in Colorado. She was stressed about being a new mother and told Doug it would be a great idea for them to get away. He agreed because somebody was going to get hurt at the rate of arguing the whole family was having. No one could see eye to eye. Doug would sometimes imagine how it would have been had he and Delanie stayed together, while Nina secretly desired to be anywhere but with Doug and the twins—not to mention the Paulas. Delanie would always say, "They all need Jesus!"

Nina left late in the evening because of one of her sorority sisters' situation. They were planning to ride together. The young lady had to cancel because of a car accident involving a close relative. Nina ended up riding alone. She never made it to the lodge. Her car was found fifty feet from an old campsite in the mountains under a canyon's ridge. According to police reports, the car was not damaged. It appeared to have been locked from the inside. This would suggest that no one was responsible for her death. Her skeletal remains did not indicate trauma or foul play.

Doug handled his emotions very well. Although, he would cry sometimes when he shared the details with Delanie. Over the last ten years, he had hardly mentioned Nina or how she died. Time truly heals. A clear conscience and a sound mind speeds up the process. Doug was and is a great father to all their children. He is a good man. He allows God to be the center of his life.

For everyone to much is given, from him much will be required.
And to whom much has been committed of him they will ask
the more. Luke 12:48 NKJV

Doug's humility and willingness to be the "clay" and His Father "be the Potter" results in so much love and many blessings to flow between him and Delanie. It overflowed into every area of their lives. Doug was able to keep so many things in check and balance. He handled the twins, Trevor and Treyvon, well. He made it easy for Delanie to accept them as her own. They call her, "Mom." She was the mother with whom they had connection. Doug and Delanie were intentional about sharing information about the twins' birth mother, and over the years, the focus was no longer about losing Nina.

God has helped the family's focus to stay on Him as He guides the lives' they are to lead. Then and now. Every day are brand new mercies. There are no shortage of experiences, tests, and victories. They are a strong family unit with a heavenly assignment, fulfilling a Godly purpose. Part of that assignment was to know when to get some help at various times in the marriage.

Be obedient when you're led to. You never know how God will use you.

The death insurance policy payments were to be released to the twins on their 21st birthday. The provisions were that they have a lawyer and a consultant to assist with investments and all other monetary matters. The twins had to be actively pursuing a degree in the study of their choice. They had to be free of any substance abuse and alcohol addictions and were not permitted to smoke any form of tobacco, marijuana, or anything associated with hookah, pipes, or rolled paper. Nina wanted her sons to be able to level-headedly handle the type of inheritance she was arranging them to have if anything happened to her. She did not want them blinded by money. Doug and her both discussed how greatly they wanted their children to succeed.

We all have witnessed people who allow themselves to fall into the traps of destruction that money, fame and/or over-achieving can bring. We have seen how all types of people and demons come out of crevices to attach themselves to those with money, fortune, and fame. The offers are overwhelming. The investment options are entrapping. The charities are plenty. The distraction is destructive. Unless you handle your time and provisions with wisdom, you may not have them long.

The twins' mother had made a noble effort to protect their sons. However, lawyers have an insatiable desire to get as much of other people's money as the law permits. The law allows them to rob you with your eyes open. The law has been known to be the primary cause of lawlessness and corruption throughout history. Lawyers study long and hard to be one step ahead of politicians. Politicians band together to create laws with amendments that do more harm than good. The wealthy reap the benefits. The poor become the burden. They both become more uncivilized.

Now Doug and Delanie would have the great pleasure of finding a lawyer and financial planner. It would be a task with risks. They truly appreciated the fact that the twins' postgraduate and/or any further education would be paid for from their inheritance. Thank you, God!

The twins naturally attracted attention—first because they were identical and handsome, secondly because they were males. The women loved them. But most importantly, they were committed to God. There's a type of energy that emits from people whom the Lord has called and chosen according to His purpose. They are magnets for both good and evil. There are others who see their inner light and feel the warmth, comfort, and healing properties it provides. Then, there are those who can't see the light because they are blinded by sinful darkness. It makes them totally uncomfortable. They naturally don't like them or want to destroy God's property because that's part of the age-old war between good versus evil or God, Who art in heaven, and the defeated foe, Satan. Both will expose what is in us.

Delanie was well aware of how toxic the twins grandfather was in the twins' mother's, Nina's, lineage. It could affect them by way of the generations. Delanie explained to Doug how important it was for them to pray specific prayers on their behalf. Doug thought she was being ridiculous and overly spiritual until one day, Trevor and Treyvon began their awareness of sexuality.

"Dad!"

"What is it?" said Doug.

"Dad!" said Trevor and Treyvon in sync. "Dad!"

"Man, if you don't stop calling me," said Doug who was now very irritated.

"Trevor is saying things that don't make no sense. He don't know what he's talking about," said Treyvon.

"I know what I'm sayin. You are just stupid," replied Trevor.

"I've told you guys to have respect for one another and have respect for yourselves," said Doug. "Why can't you have conversations without name calling? Why are you calling me? I used to referee for your games, but those days are long gone. You both are now teenagers acting younger than your sister. Act your age!"

"But, Dad, we were talking about girls, and Trevor said that age is just a number and he can get it on with his teacher Ms. Keys if he wanted to because when they get older, they will both be in their twenties and it won't be that much of an age difference. He thinks his body is in shape for her. He's taller than her."

Doug thought to himself, *Here we go again.* He had to clear up many misconceptions over the last few years. He was so glad Delanie and their daughter, Dionne, were not home. The twins were now arguing back and forth. "Time out, time out, man!" yelled Doug in order to silence them. "Man, you don't have to argue back and forth. You state your view. Listen, then reason. No one person is completely right, and no one person is 100 percent wrong. There is something to learn from one another. Always remember to be calm in order to get your point across. How can you hear each other if you are angry and uptight? It's not that deep, guys," said Doug.

Treyvon, the oldest, began slowly taking into account what his father had just explained. He was the more level-headed twin. He said, "Trevor was approached by his teacher, Ms. Keys. She said, 'If you were much older, I would be your significant other.'

She thought I didn't hear her. But, I did, Dad. She's always watching us, even at our ball games. I want to report her, but Trevor likes her and won't back me up if I report her to the principal."

Doug sat down for this one. He asked, "Trevor, is this true?"

"No, Dad," Trevor sighed. "Treyvon always takes things the wrong way. What can I say if the woman wants me? I look good."

Doug replied, "Trevor, this is serious." Doug had just contradicted himself. He thought is wasn't "that deep." Excuse me for saying it's not that deep. It is. This woman is there to teach you in a dignified manner. She is not to make innuendos or any type of advances on a fifteen-year-old. You are a minor. She can get suspended and even arrested.

She can cause you to view life in a poisonous way. I raised you guys to be responsible. I hope she's not married or twice your age."

"She is, Dad," interrupted Treyvon. "But she's around twenty-five."

"Oh, I'm going to handle this," said Doug, who was now fuming.

"Dad, why would Trevor even look at our teacher? There are plenty of honeys our age," asked Treyvon.

Doug began to preach. "Don't call them that. You call your wife, 'honey,' when you get one, prayerfully, years from now. I've told you both, if you don't show respect for and responsibility with young ladies, you won't have my permission to spend time with them. I know your hormones might be telling you that you are men ready for a relationship. But prove it to me. I believe in purity before marriage. I am against dating multiple girls looking for sexual connections. You need to be reminded that you two are raised as Christians, God's chosen, future representatives of God's kingdom to a lost, dying world. Your whole identity is to live a God-conscious life—leading, teaching, and showing others who Jesus is. You are not to prey on girls, women, or your teacher. You are to pray for them or with them in a secure manner following God's lead. You will not travel the road I traveled or the roads my father, your mother's father, and any weak-minded male we know has traveled. I'm so apologetic for the behavior of males across this globe when we do not appreciate what God has given us. We are nothing without God. Every time we think about a woman in the wrong way, it brings strife and discord in our home, man. Look at you both arguing and being separated because of this Ms. Keys. I got the keys, *alright*—the key to a long prosperous life is to keep your mind on our great Heavenly Father, and if you have a problem doing that, then keep your eyes on me. I'm visible, upfront, and willing to guide you with God's power in me. That's exactly what I'm here for. God designed it this way. He, also, designed a man for a woman. She is to be his wife. Same-sex relationships and marriages are unacceptable in the sight of God. Homosexuality is a dysfunction in society for those who like sin more than honoring our Savior, Jesus. Like most people, homosexuals lack self-control of their minds and bodies. They are lost souls. However, God still loves them. We are to help them heal and be delivered. You or I won't have the power or the will if we are traveling down "sin lane" ourselves. Just the thought of you looking at a girl or woman with sexual desires is not good for you. It affects you negatively. It affects all of us, including the female you are lusting for because that's not love. You can cause the female to have ill feelings for you and be reciprocal in her lust for you. Don't encourage sin, man. This goes for both of you.This may seem like a playful, even small thing. But it ends up hurting so many, including Mrs. Keys, her husband, and her family. How important is it to you Trevor? You will have self-control. Use the power of the Holy Spirit to help you. It will cut down on the mess in this world if everyone obeys the leading of the Holy One." Douglas went on to say, "You both have a wife specifically designed for you. You will definitely know when she crosses your path. I have prayed to God for years for it to be clear to you both. I got sidetracked years ago when I listened to your grandmother and your Aunt Paula about who I should be with and who I should marry. They did not have a relationship with God. They were wrong about their choice concerning your mother, Nina, as I have shared with you before. It turned out for good because I am with your mom, Delanie, my beautiful wife who loves me and you, too. But look what happened in between. Your birth mother did not get the privilege to raise you. She loved you, and I got the most rewarding sons anyone could ask for. Don't let your family down, guys. Know that Ms. Keys or any other person is not worth you having separation from God."

"Preach!" smirked the twins simultaneously.

Doug wasn't quite done. He smiled and said, "Age is not just a number. Age dictates when you go to school, what grade you will be in, when you are legal to drive, when you are eligible to get Social Security retirement, when your body changes...Ms. Keys won't be that appealing to you when you have to get a full-time job to put money in her prison account because she's in jail for seducing a minor or when she can't live in certain neighborhoods because of her criminal record. She won't be able to live less than 500 feet from any school, library, or park. Is that the kind of future you want, son? Change your thinking, yet?"

Trevor humbly looked at his father. "Yes, I feel you, Dad."

"Thank you, Treyvon, for loving your family enough to bring this to our attention," said Doug. "Both of you be patient and wait until you get married under God's blessing to the young lady close to your age. You will be able to grow together, relate better with one another, and have similar interests. Believe me. A woman going through "the change of life" with a young man going through puberty is no match."

Treyvon and Trevor said simultaneously, "What's the change of life and puberty have to do with it?"

"My point exactly!" exclaimed their father. "That's another conversation for another time. Let's pray, Princes."

Doug led. "My God, my Heavenly Father. I give You all the honor. You hold my sons and I in Your embrace. You have given us the privilege of a calling that is more than we could ask or think. We accept our calling with reverence to Your Holy Son. We accept Your peace, protection, and provision to carry out our assignments. Forgive us for any sins, transgressions, or iniquities we may have or will commit. We forgive Ms. Keys for her wrongdoing. We know that she will not be allowed to do Trevor and Treyvon any harm because they are covered by the blood of Jesus. We call her behavior into subjection. We bind the work of the enemy. We loose victory in every area of our lives and our family. We cover my wife and daughter. Bless the women of the earth. If God be for us, what can stand against? We pray Psalm 91 over us, our loved ones, and the world. Thank you for giving your angels charge over us. In Jesus's matchless name we pray…"

Altogether they agreed, "Amen."

Delanie was involved with her husband in the writing of a formal letter to the principal and school board. Ms. Keys was suspended upon further investigation and later quietly left her position.

Doug's prayers for their children were so detailed. They led to an hour or more of his petitions being made known to God. Delanie loved it and loved her husband all the more for listening to her advice on the matter. An Ephesians-charactered man raising Ephesians young men is a beautiful thing. Let's not forget all the benefits this will bring their daughter. She will, in turn, see and learn to appreciate her husband. Prayerfully, she will have firsthand, up close, and personal experiences that will result in healthy relationships with those of the opposite sex. The respect and adoration of the men in her life will bring favor and blessings for years to come. She will identify with males with a healthy perspective, even when they fall short of being strong, role models. Because they love the Lord and poured into Dionne, we'll believe so will she. With the family prayers and continual belief that this will be their story and experience, so shall it be. It lines up with the promises of God to those who love Him.

Delanie can attest to the effectual, fervent prayers of the righteous availing much. One of the twins, Treyvon, seemed to have temporarily lost his mind when Dionne was around six or seven. She was in the bathroom with the door slightly ajar. She had just gotten out of the shower. Her little under developed body should not have been appealing, attractive, nor enticing to anyone. Treyvon was coming upstairs and saw her. He did not choose to close the door. He did not choose to just keep walking. No, he chose to peek in on her. This was his baby sister, whether they were a blended family or not. Delanie came out of her and Doug's bedroom. She witnessed him looking at his sister in a slightly creeping low position. Here he was around seventeen with hormones raging, looking at their baby girl. *Not on my watch*, Delanie said to herself.

She bumped him really hard with her hip, knocking him over. He hit his head on the the doorknob, then landed on the floor hard. "I'm so sorry, Treyvon" said Delanie as not to alarm Dionne. Delanie was being intentional not to let Dionne in on what appeared to be future pedophilic behavior. She closed the bathroom door, helped Treyvon peel himself off of the floor, and led him into her and Doug's bedroom. Delanie checked his head for any open cuts. There didn't appear to be any physical damage. She went into their bathroom and ran cold water on a towel. She led him into their oversized sitting area. Treyvon sat down slowly. Delanie believed his feelings were more affected then his head. She asked him how he felt. He closed his eyes and shook his head, yes, as if to signal that he was okay.

Delanie rinsed her hands in a fragrant, therapeutic oil. She used oil to place on those who were in need of an extra touch from God. It was her "holy oil," which helped break the effects of sin and empowered anointing, both symbolically and spiritually. She touched her son's head, then held both of his outreached hands. Treyvon knew what she was doing. This was a practice their family was familiar with. "Submit to God; resist the devil," she said. "Help us, Lord, to stand strong. Deliver us from evil." A short but powerful prayer to a mighty God.

God delivered. Treyvon never gave any indication of an unhealthy interest in his sister again. He never defended himself with maybe, "I was going to play a trick on her."

Treyvon was the master of pranks. Once while his brother was sleeping, he put shaving cream in his brother's hand, then tickled his brother's nose. We all know how that turned out! Perhaps, he had originally been intending to prank his sister but another spirit crept in. Delanie was not entirely sure. In Treyvon's mind, he wasn't sure what happened, especially after his head had hit the doorknob. The twins' grandfather's demons would not be permitted to manifest in Delanie's sons or her daughter, for that matter. Delanie wasn't having it. There were times when the twins would say, "We won't follow in our grandfather's ways, Mom and Dad." Doug had given them the history of their grandfather's weakness when Doug was teaching them about iniquity versus transgressions versus sins.

We all sin and fall short of the glory of God. There are different levels we can cross into. These three terms communicate the same idea of evil and lawlessness.

Sin means to miss the mark, falling short of God's standard. This violation is knowingly and/or unknowingly. Transgression is to go beyond boundaries intentionally, lawlessness, choosing to disobey, blatant disregard for authority. This is purposely sinning *(see Ex. 10:16)*. Iniquity is more deeply rooted. It's practicing evil without repentance *(see Rev. 17:4)*. This one leads to no fear of God, abomination until no repentance is possible.

Doug had no choice but to use their grandfather's story to make it more real to them. The truth had to come to light, which would allow all of them to go forth with liberty and freedom.

Fighting our demons has always been an ongoing battle for mankind. It's so important to read history. It's even more important to study His Story. By this, I mean Jesus's story. The Bible is all about Jesus from the beginning to the end. It truly is a love story between God and His creation. As in all relationships, there will be highs and lows, not to mention conflict, strife, and hardships. But know that the end of everything leads right to God and new beginnings.

In true awareness, you'll see most relationships start with a good idea. They start with a plan for something beautiful. There's hope, belief, vision, and a dream. They make you feel good about yourself and others. Infatuation. Let's be clear. Infatuation is not the same as love. Love is much more than that. God is love. God is not infatuation. There are those who put more merit on being in love or infatuated. They will destroy God's plan for their lives, their marriage, their family because they feel they are "not in love" with him or her anymore. This is a wake-up call. True love is not determined how infatuated or in love with someone you are. True love is more concrete. True love is sacrificial. True love is when you love God with all you heart, mind, body, and soul. Then you will be given the ability to love others that way, specifically your spouse.

Did the twins' grandmother, Karen (Nina's mother) love their grandfather, Nathan (Nina's father)? No. Neither of them had a personal relationship with God. Oh, they went to church several times a year. As we are well aware, going to church does not solidify your relationship with God.

Jesus answered him, "Most assuredly, I say to you, unless one is born again he cannot see the kingdom of God. John 3:3 NKIV

The kingdom of heaven is like a man who sowed good seed in his field. But while everyone was sleeping, his enemy came, and sowed weeds among the wheat, and went away.

When the wheat sprouted and formed heads, then the weeds also appeared.

The owner's servants came to him and said, "Sir, didn't you sow good seed in your field? Where then did the weeds come from?.

An enemy did this, he replied. The servants asked him, "do you want us to go and pull them up?" "No" he answered, "because While you are pulling the weeds, you may uproot the wheat with them. Let both grow together until the harvest. At that time I will tell the harvesters; first collect the weeds and tie them in bundles to be burned, then gather the wheat and bring it into my barn. Matthew 13:24-30 NIV

The Parable re: separating His true Christians followers/ believers from the counterfeit Christian who are Satan followers.

Karen gave her life to Jesus Christ after repenting and allowing Him to change her heart.

She has a strong and faithful relationship with God these days. It shows in her choices. It shows in her ability to be obedient and committed to her faith. God has placed His Spirit in her, and she has accepted it. It shows in her eyes and in her heart. She has a hope and a future, despite all those dark, lonely nights she spent in the guest bedroom while her then-husband Nathan was slowly overtaken by the evil spirit of lust.

It began with his wanting to experience and try immoral sexual positions with her. He wanted her to engage in uncomfortable sexual activity more and more. It moved over into his staying up late watching pornography for hours until masturbation would no longer satisfy him. The pornography imprinted on someone's soul lasts much longer than any drug or alcohol addiction. It is equally as poisonous.

He had feelings of wanting other men but never acted on it. Finally, he found a new greed. When Nina would come home from volleyball practice with a few of her friends who thought Nina's dad was "kinda cute," he and Satan had the sick desire to spread the poison into those young lives, all strategically to destroy each and every one of them.

If I get the head of the family, the house will be divided. A house divided will fall—then I'll roam into the next open house. This is one of the strategies of the enemy. People fall for it more than we know. Churches all over the globe have been infested and affected by this same age-old trap and tactic of Satan and his kind. *Believers, we are the church.*

GOD
(Always keep His principles and focus on His kingdom)

Identity:

Plan:

You
(place your name here)

Purpose:

Priorities:

Prayer:

Vision:

* Pray first, then use the ability to listen before completing

A blueprint for the church:

GOD'S PLAN

Identity: I am the son/daughter of God. For Men: I am the leader/head of my family. For women: I am co leader of my family. Both: My body is the temple of the Holy One. I am the "bride" of God. I am called according to His purpose through Jesus Christ.

Plan: I will trust and obey God. I will seek first God's kingdom and all His righteousness so that I can carry out my true purpose. I will obtain all the fruits of the Spirit(love, joy, peace(not anger), kindness, gentleness, goodness, long-suffering, self-control, most importantly faithfulness. True relationship with God, knowing His Word.

Purpose: To serve God first and then serve others. Believe. Seek God's help so that I can teach, spiritually lead, provide, protect others as unto the Lord.

Priorities: God, spouse, children, family, church/church family, ministry, work, school, hobbies, etc.

Prayer: I confess all my wrongs, I admit my failures, and I repent to you Lord, Jesus. Help me to live according to your Word. I surrender. I will pray these Scriptures: John 3:16, Matt 6:33, I Cor 7:14, Mal 2 & 3, Mk 16-17 (*& Pray Scriptures that God personally places on your heart.)*

Vision: To be filled with the Holy Spirit operating in God's kingdom using my gifts to edify God, guide my family and others, do His Will not mine. Not conforming to this world. Be transformed and help raise up a new standard. Appreciate all that God has given me. Believe and receive the blessing of life and life more abundantly.

Nathan could have stopped the evil. He could have sought his Heavenly Father. He should have surrendered to God, not his selfish weaknesses. He should have prayed for help and believed that his prayers would be answered. He should have sought professional counseling and therapy to overcome pedophilia, pornography, and pride. He should have watched good television and video material. He and his wife needed healing.

His behavior affected Karen deeply. She couldn't believe what was happening. She went into survival mode to protect Nina and herself the only way she knew how to. Nathan slept with over twenty young girls, some as young as thirteen years of age. This practice lasted for six years. While, Karen fell into deeper depression, she picked up a few demons of her own. She had thoughts of suicide, then homicide. She made plans to have Nathan killed. All attempts failed. God had a better plan. God had a better consequence for Nathan. God allowed him to live—to live with much pain and suffering. God did not allow his seed to reproduce in any of Nathan's young victims. Karen believed if she exposed him, their reputation would be severed for life. She did not have adequate proof to give besides her statement. Karen did not work or know how to drive. Nathan had helped reduce her so low that she had lost sight, hope, and purpose, just to name a few. She was overtaken by the darkness, and no one but God could bring her out of the pit.

Nathan no longer had a soul nor did he care. When things are at the lowest, it is the perfect opportunity for God to do the impossible. This was a recipe for God to enter in.

Satan is synonymous with death and destruction. But God gives life and life more abundantly. Karen is living for the Lord. Nathan is no longer able to walk or talk. He barely has control over his bladder. He has limited physical activity. Perhaps one day he will no longer suffer so much pain. Perhaps one day he will totally surrender and die—die to himself. He was delivered from some of his demons after Nina passed, but God knows the heart. Perhaps he will have a change of heart, cry out to the Lord, and be saved from eternal death. And if he can't cry out, perhaps he will believe it in his heart and write it down.

Doug shared a protected version of Nathan's testimony to their children. He was thoughtful of the impact it would have if it were too detailed. Actually, Nathan's past is what prompted Doug and Delanie to have a conversation about seeking counseling. Delanie understood Doug's concern. She was not willing to let yet another entity in their lives. This would be yet another appointment to keep, another person to associate with, and another person probing in their lives, digging up old bones and uncovering wounds. Doug could not have known the secret places of Delanie's mind where she would sometimes be reminded of the Paula(s) influence and Doug's choice to get involved with Nina and her generational curses. Delanie would run down the list of what ifs, the couldas. The shouldas would leave an emptiness inside. She did not want to expose their children or anyone for that matter. Delanie did not want Doug to know her feelings. She did not want to open old wounds or get more scars. These emotions couldn't be categorized as fear. Perhaps, fear had some element to them—more so than not. Most importantly, it was the nature of a mother/wife to want to protect her husband and her "cubs."

That's exactly why she sought the Lord without hesitation. Her relationship with her Father Who Art in Heaven was what kept her emotions in check. Conferring with Him allowed her to have a sound mind. This would enhance the fruit of Spirit better known as self-control. She would be the last one to openly claim this fruit of the Spirit was fully ripe in her and that she used it daily. It was still being developed.

Galatians 5:22

Delanie would soon be reminded that she had to renew her mind. She needed to look at things the way God would. There's always a much bigger picture than any human mind can comprehend. There are little treasures to pick up along this journey. God gives us life and definitely life more abundantly. We must not always focus on the natural when trying to avoid the inevitable, even when it makes us uncomfortable. Doug would say to her, "We must get out of our comfort coves so we can see the glory of God at work." Oooo...Delanie loved it when her husband operated in wisdom. He got it from his Father—not the earthly one, the Heavenly One. That's where true comfort lies.

"Dr. Fulton? Your 4:00 appointment has arrived. I'll have Mrs. Revel be seated." said the receptionist.

"Thank you, Carla," replied Dr. Fulton. She then took a deep breath. It had now been weeks since the sessions with the Revels had begun. For the life of Dr. Fulton, she could not see what Doug saw in Delanie. She also wondered why this couple left her feeling uneasy after their sessions. The schedule with them together was coming to a close. They had moved into the part of counseling where they were required to be seen individually. They were scheduled to have two additional sessions where they would be joined for a closing evaluation.

Dr. Fulton was very concise in this process. She was rated by the Board of Psychological Studies Institute as one of the top in her field. She came very highly recommended. Her sessions with the Revels moved very quickly without too many setbacks. However, with all her experience, she felt something was affecting her that was beyond her understanding—a pulling on her strength.

"Dr. Fulton? Your 4:00 pm appointment has arrived," said Carla sensing that there was a preoccupation in the doctor that she'd never noticed before. Mrs. Revel had already been told to have a seat, and she was waiting in the reception area. Later, Dr. Fulton welcomed Delanie in her office.

Dr. Sarai Fulton had her office decorated with very good taste. The colors made you feel comfortable with a burst of hopefulness. Today, the colors could not govern the feel in the atmosphere. It was not warm between Delanie and Dr. Fulton.

Dr. Fulton said, "Hello, Mrs. Revel."

"Hi, Dr. Fulton," said Delanie.

Dr. Fulton began with, "Time is moving really quickly. We have been meeting twice a week for some time now. Actually, it has been twelve weeks since we began. I believe we have made great progress. I have met with you both jointly and individually. As I listen to you both, I find there are resentments that have been severed. I notice you both have changed your perspectives. You, Mrs. Revel, have moved from a negative view of professional counseling, psychologists, and psychiatrists. I clearly understand your apprehension when it applies to unprofessional ones in the field whose practices are not healthy by any measure. They can give us all a bad name. Hopefully, our experience here has given you a new respect for what we do here. I will now recommend we return to our once-a-week sessions with both of you. I find individual sessions are no longer needed because you have really grown and healed in many areas. Wouldn't you agree, Mrs. Revel?"

Delanie would agree. Delanie had learned over these twelve weeks to enjoy the moments. She had decreased in her "overthinking a thing." She accepted the fact that Dr. Fulton wasn't a bad person, just a spiritually lost soul. Dr. Fulton absolutely did not need to see Delanie's bold and sometimes disrespectful attitude. Delanie was a beautiful child of God who was once lost in a world of foolishness and sin herself. She had always known of God but did not have a true relationship with King Jesus. Oh, but now she did and was to be an ambassador, a representative of a kingdom that is all about love—true love. Delanie needed to reflect love in her walk, talk, and thinking. The world is watching and expects a true Christian to be well-behaved always. But, today was not that day. Delanie was still in a fleshly body. Her spirit, like so many followers of Christ, was constantly in battle with the body. How could any Christian get anyone to know this is how it will be until Jesus returns? Especially, those who don't believe in God or Jesus. Like yours truly, the doctor.

"Yes, Dr. Sarai, I would agree," sighed Delanie.

Dr. Fulton was ready to correct her with her preference to be called Dr. Fulton. Delanie would not let her get a word in. Delanie continued, "I will agree that I've grown because I've allowed you in my life and my family's history, but I've not seen or received a healthy response from you until today. How can you, week after week, "get to know me" and I'm not allowed to call you by your first name? You have my husband and I come here, and you won't explore the part of our lives that is most sacred and dear to us. It is truly hard for me to accept the advice and recommendations from someone who doesn't have a clue of who we serve, who we represent, what our purposes are, and what the ultimate plan for our lives' really is. You are educated to access and evaluate others. Do you ever evaluate yourself and your relationships? We didn't just happen to come to you for help without you, in turn, receiving and learning from us. Yes, you will get money for your services, but you will also get a lesson from each and every person you treat. You need to be very aware of and watch how you treat each and every person—especially while addressing their individual, and if they are married, collective needs. My husband and I have needs that you refuse to explore because you don't want to talk about our religious beliefs. It is absolutely a huge part of who we are. Since you accepted us as clients, it was your professional duty to learn or at least research what we find so near and dear to us. But closed-mindedness will divide people every time. We have been divinely placed in your life, Dr. Sarai. I want to call you by name because names are very significant. They hold meaning and purpose. You have the same name as the wife of Abraham, who was a man devoted to God. God promised to make nations from them as many as the stars, the ones in the sky. Your name means "she that strives," and it also means "a princess." Sarai in the Bible had striking beauty.

Kings of peoples shall be of her. Genesis 17:16 (NKJV)

The promise to "make nations from you" was promised to a woman who could not have children. Sarai (Sarah), in the Bible, laughed at God in her younger years but later conceived and gave birth to a baby boy at the age of 90. Her husband, Abraham, was 100 years old. And you most likely don't believe any of what's in the Bible," Delanie relented. "I'll pray for you, Dr. Sarai." Delanie was feeling exhausted but continued. "You can't fully treat a couple or anyone unless you know who you are. The only way that's possible is if you know the One who created you. You must begin to think differently, dearest Doctor. You may have never personally met the people who designed a curriculum. But you trust and even use it. You trust who may have written the books that led to your getting the academic achievements you have obtained. You, ultimately, use this knowledge in your practice. But you won't make the time, let alone have the desire, to know who made both you and them. You believe that you, solely, have the substance and power to heal or treat your clients/patients, causing them to be whole individuals after your sessions. When in fact, that is completely absurd thinking because you're not whole yourself. In truth, you must be teachable to teach others. You don't have the credentials to counsel a married couple effectively without your willingness to be married to the One who created marriage. You must recognize God is the Creator of all things. You must accept that His Son, Jesus, is the only way to have a relationship with God, the Father. You must believe you are unable to do anything without them. You may be equipped with a title, some BA, MBA, or other three digits of the alphabet behind your name, but know that God is the Alpha. And you can bet your life on that. He's the Omega, too. At the end of the day, Dr. Sarai, you are one of God's creations whom He loves and wants you to know and love Him. We, Doug and I, have been strategically placed in your life. We are on your patient role, intercepting your path like a fork in the road, bringing you to deliverance and a relationship with God the Father, God the Son, and God the Holy Spirit. Believe it or not, it's your choice. But it must be…" Delanie paused, "no…**it is time for you and your husband to choose to worship and serve GOD.** It's for you and your husband's good."

Dr. Fulton was totally paralyzed, unable to speak. It was right where God needed her to be.

Delanie continued. "I don't need human's accolades and rewards to qualify me to say and disclose what I'm sharing. We all need the divine knowledge that only comes from God. And please don't focus or be fooled by the way God is getting His message to you. It looks like it's coming from me—yes, the one you thought that my husband, Doug, was crazy to be married to.

Me, the one you had many adjectives to describe when talking to your husband and peers. Me, the one you felt you needed an alcoholic drink after our sessions. The doctor did not know that Delanie had the gift of prophecy.

"You have it twisted, Dr. Sarai. I'm the very one to give you this message. You won't receive this message by attending any of God's houses around this globe. I understand you and your husband are well-traveled, but what I'm blessing you with is by God's grace. His mercy happening right here in your office. After all those wasted opportunities to love and serve Him, I only hope you see how this is more valuable than any vacation or trip around the world. Now, perhaps, you will understand why I talk a lot. I have much to say. It's because I serve a matchless Heavenly God so there will always be limitless information and knowledge. Right here, right now, Dr. Sarai. Until you get the knowing, by faith, of the One who created you, you won't be able to be whole. Do it by faith, Dr. Sarai, not just your feelings. Will you give your life to Christ by admitting you need a Savior, confess with your mouth and believe in your heart that Jesus is Lord and died and rose for you, and from this day forward, will you allow Him in your life?

Dr. Fulton was quiet. Tears rolled down.

Delanie continued. "Dr. Sarai? I need you to know this is so much bigger than we can imagine. With all the knowledge in the history books, with all the studies doctors/ scientists/"great minds" have participated in and technology, we still don't have all the answers. We, in the kingdom of God love with the Love of the Lord. Therefore, I love you and want you to live. You will live the life only Christ can provide. You have no idea how many gifts, talents, and abilities He gives to those who serve Him. Sometimes, He gives it to those who do not believe in Him only to serve His purpose. You have no idea of who and what

Doug and I are called to accomplish in the lives of others. Do not be deceived by what we appear to be or not be, to have or not to have."

Dr. Fulton had no idea how gifted the woman who was sitting before her was, nor did she know Delanie had been given insight into future occurrences. She was anointed.

Delanie humbled herself and gently asked again. "Will you give your life to Jesus Christ, admitting you need Him, asking Him for forgiveness? Will you confess with your mouth and believe in your heart that Jesus is Lord? He gave His life for ours so that we would be free from death and destruction. He died for us. Will you live for Him?"

There were not enough tissues in the room, let alone the tissue box.

Dr. Sarai said, "Yes. Yes, I believe I need Jesus. I confess I'm a sinner, and I believe He will save me, save my husband." More tears followed. "Jesus! Thank you for saving me." Dr. Sarai Fulton gave her life and soul to Jesus Christ that day.

Delanie cried out, "Counselor...that's you, Lord!" She hugged Dr. Sarai and said to her, "Counselor, may I introduce you to the one and only true Counselor, the Triune God." The Holy Spirit took up residence.

"Mrs. Revel, you can call me Dr. Sarai," said Dr. Fulton.

Delanie said, "Please call me, Delanie." They both were crying. Another stronghold broken. Another healing took place. Another healthy relationship formed. God's glory will prevail. These two beautiful daughters of Christ will share this part of their experience for years to come.

Delanie was so excited. Dr. Sarai had answered the call on her life. This would make it a little easier when she would be able to reveal to Dr. Sarai that she would be like Abraham's Sarai in the Bible. Dr. Sarai, too, had a barren womb. Despite the doctors' diagnosis, she would be delivering her first baby boy in seven months. God had revealed this to Delanie. *Thank you, Father.*

Again He said to me, "Prophesy to these bones, and say to them, "O dry bones, hear the word of the Lord! Thus says the Lord God to these bones. Surely I will cause breath to enter into you and you shall live." Ezekiel 37:4-5 NKJV

While driving home, Delanie wondered if God would have her share with Dr. Sarai some of her own Bible-like stories, stories where her own life reflected some the stories on those supernatural pages. Delanie could actually relate to the love triangle in the book of Genesis (in the Bible). This testimony surrounds Jacob. Jacob's uncle, Laban, influenced and manipulated Jacob into marrying Leah (Laban's elder daughter) instead of Rachel (Laban's younger daughter). Jacob adored and desired Rachel, not Leah. Delanie reflected on the similarity of how the two Paulas had tried to influence her own husband to marry Nina, knowing how he loved Delanie. Although, Doug never married Nina, they interrupted Delanie and Doug's union. Just as Doug truly loved Delanie, Jacob truly loved Rachel. They both were finally with the wife they were destined to have.

Genesis chapters 29-30

However, Doug and Delanie were not first cousins like Jacob and his wife/wives were.

The conflict between their offspring would not be anything like Jacob's offspring.

Prayerfully, Delanie was determined that would not happen in her situation. How awful was it in 2 Samuel chapter 11, when King David used his authority and manipulative power to steal another man's (Uriah's) wife. King David's lust superseded his judgment. Doug's desires superseded his judgment when he, too, manipulated Delanie, knowing she loved and had plans to marry her first love and high school sweetheart.

Just like Bathsheba, Delanie's first conceived child was a male. Delanie miscarried. King David and Bathsheba's firstborn died, was struck down. Someone died for these unions to happen. Both had similar losses but different outcomes. Although they were a different set of circumstances, the lessons to be learned are profound. The consequences were powerful.

Delanie knew how Bathsheba had felt losing a child. She could empathize. Bathsheba suffered more deeply because her husband (Uriah) was killed at the request of her second husband (King David), and the consequences went longer and deeper for David and Bathsheba.

2 Samuel 13

Delanie was reminded of when one of the twins inappropriately watched his sister get dressed. *But God and I handled that*, thought Delanie. It resonated with Delanie how Amnon (in the Bible) was sickly in lust for his sister, Tamar. Knowing this prompted Delanie to pray. She prayed her and Doug's blended family would not mirror David and Bathsheba's family with that type of dysfunction. And like David, who went on to be restored to God exceedingly above what was imagined, Doug had, too. Doug was more on fire for God and the things of His kingdom than what one could imagine.

To be chosen to be a mouthpiece for God, as Delanie had, results in experiencing very challenging circumstances. Be assured that you will always be victorious. God has His hand on you! It marvels us to this very day when a human being actually hears from God. It's not usually in an audible voice but often in a motion in the brainwaves that detect incoming information. This information is downloaded into your mind. It reaches your conscience and sometimes sends a wave of emotion through your body. Those who are spiritual and know the things of God know it's the Holy Spirit because they clearly did not think of it on their own. The process is not always easy to explain. Other times, you may be given a revelation while you are sleeping, and you may wake up knowing what to do or say. A better term is "dropped in your spirit."

Incline your ear, and come to Me. Hear, and your soul shall live.
And I will make an everlasting covenant with you——-the sure
mercies of David.
Isaiah 55:3 NKJV

So shall My Word be that goes forth from My mouth; It shall not
return to Me void. But, it will accomplish what I please and it
Shall prosper in the thing for which I sent it.
Isaiah 55:11 NKJV

For My thoughts are not your thoughts nor are your ways My
ways, says the Lord.
Isaiah 55:9 NLT

God ways are not like ours. Receiving instruction and/or hearing the voice of God is definitely not limited to these forms of communication from our Heavenly Father. The adversary (Satan) is capable of deceiving us with a mock version of communicating to our spirits.

Delanie had been seasoned to hear God's voice. He had given her insight into many people's lives. Sometimes she was given permission to share this knowledge, and other times, she was not.

Delanie was hesitant to share what she had been shown regarding Dr. Sarai.

Dr. Sarai picked up her $900 iPhone and texted a message to her husband. It read: "Honey, I am so excited! I have some news you will not believe."

Adam replied via text, "Shoot" (in other words "tell me").

Dr. Sarai wrote, "I've given myself to Christ."

He texted back, "Who's Christ...are you cheating on me?"

Dr. Sarai replied with an "okay" emoji. Then she texted, "I'll meet you at Sando's Café in an hour."

Adam was pulling up to Sando's Café at the same time his wife, Sarai, pulled into the crowded parking lot. Sando's Café was usually crowded on Fridays. It was Thursday.

Perhaps there was a special party venue for someone's birthday. Sarai found a parking spot on the end row near the entrance. However, Adam could only find a parking spot in the adjoining restaurant's parking lot. It took them a few moments to reach one another. Lately, for some reason, they both had had this insatiable desire for one another. It was almost like they were in the early period of their marriage. It was somewhat unexplainable but fully exciting. They embraced for some time, maybe 5-15 minutes. Who was counting in this moment? Perhaps it was Dr. Sarai's newly-found relationship with Jesus Christ.

When they entered the restaurant, it was crowded, as they expected because of no available parking in the lot. Adam gave the hostess their name. Surprisingly, they were seated quickly. "What's this I hear about giving yourself to Christ?" began Adam.

"Honey, I know! I know how it must sound. I'm elated. It's like something I cannot fully interpret or explain," Sarai continued. "You also would not believe who revealed the need for me to have a personal relationship with God. It was only a matter of time."

Sarai's face lit up. Her inner spirit was beaming. Her beautiful husband, she thought, had to feel what was emitting from her soul. And he did. Sarai looked deeply into her husband's eyes. She continued, "Remember, when we went to that conference in the mountains years ago? The speaker was a Christian. His name was Larry Jennings or something."

Adam corrected her, "Larry Bennings."

"Yes," she agreed. "He was teaching on success in every area of your life, but it all stems from our Creator who reveals Himself as God the Father, God the Son, and God the Holy Spirit. Well, God the Son is Jesus Christ. Jesus Christ is who intercepted the destruction and death of us all by sacrificing His life so that we could be reconnected to His Father and live and not die. We are to live in the freedom, the liberty, and the favor that Jesus gives us. That's why I chose to live for Him—doing His will, His way."

There was an unusual expression on Adam's face. He was absorbing her words. Sarai said, "You remember that couple who I took as my patients in March, the Revels? The wife, so humbly but intentionally, offered me the gift of life. I gave my thoughts, my cares, my heart, and my soul to Jesus Christ." Tears of joy flowed from her eyes.

The birthday party at the back of the restaurant loudly gave a cheer because their loved one had now joined the celebration for whom they were waiting for her to arrive. The group was singing "Happy Birthday" very loudly— so much so that Adam and Sarai could no longer communicate. They decided to leave. The waiter had only provided their beverages and had not taken their order yet. Adam left a small tip. They headed to Sarai's car.

They got to the car and decided to sit inside to decide an alternate place to eat and talk. Adam wanted to continue to listen to what his wife was saying earlier about God.

"Wow, what a noisy party. Well, it shows how much they really care for that young lady," said Sarai. "That's what I'm experiencing as we speak. I feel the tender love of God, Adam. I want you to experience this, His presence."

"Honey, I love you. But, I'm not sure of the whole God thing. Organized religion is not for me. I don't want you to be deceived, either. We are doing just fine. We have our practices. We have a beautiful home. We vacation wherever we want every year…" Adam trailed off for a moment as if he was hearing himself talk, but somehow, it was a bunch of irrelevant comments. "We have each other." He ended with that.

Sarai spoke, "And now we will have the most important piece of life—that's Christ. We have those things. They are worthless in comparison to life and freedom with God. We must make serving Him our priority. This so much bigger than we know. Let's research this, honey. We've gone to school, read books by various authors, and attended colleges for years. Yet we have not studied the Bible. Will you join me in this new life that I'm willing to lead?" she almost pleaded.

Adam looked at her. It felt like he was beginning to feel compelled to take on this brilliance that his wife was handing him. He didn't know that Delanie and her prayer partners were praying for them across town at that very moment.

Adam said, "Yes! How can I not accept what my gorgeous lady is trying to teach me?"

For God so loved the world that He gave His only begotten Son, that whoever believes in Him should not perish but, have everlasting life.
John 3:16 NKJV

He continued, "I trust you, so I'm willing to research with you. I see a glow all over you, baby. Let's do this and later do the other thing..." As he leaned in to kiss his wife, they both could hear rap music blaring from a black SUV that was sitting on 20-inch rims *Boom, boom!* Adam could feel the base from the sound system in the SUV. The vehicle was coming their way fast. Adam began to say, "Why is he driving..." That was all he could get out of his mouth before the SUV crashed into the rear of Sarai's car. It was turning to get into a parking spot before someone else did. Neither Adam or Sarai had on seat belts because they were not in motion. Sarai's head jerked forward then back. Adam's head hit hers as he was attempting to kiss and love on his wife. Silence was in the air.

The driver of the SUV got out. His airbag had deployed. He grabbed his cell phone, called 9-1-1, then collapsed. People ran out from the restaurant and nearby businesses. It was an immediate response from the fire department and rescue teams. Sarai was unconscious. Adam was slightly bleeding from the lip and cheek. They were rushed to the hospital. Sarai came to consciousness in the ambulance with Adam at her side. The EMT assured her she would be okay. She might have a little headache, the EMT warned, but nothing fatal. They were taking her vitals, and, surprisingly, they looked good.

They arrived at the hospital. The emergency team did not have to be on high alert. Sarai had a gash on her forehead, and her earlobe was bleeding from the collision with Adam's teeth when they were hit. The doctors decided to run tests and watch her for the next twenty-four hours and believed she would be released the following day as long as her vitals remained normal.

Adam was examined and released. He decided to stay the night with Sarai. He kissed her and assured her he would go handle the car accident situation. He planned to return afterwards.

The nurse offered Sarai pain medication. For some reason, Sarai refused it. Adam pulled the nurse aside and gave her permission to give her something with low milligrams because he believed his wife would need something to relax. He thought she was startled and maybe a little out of it. The nurse went to get the medication then, immediately, was called to the ICU for a high alert trauma call.

A young lady who had come to visit another patient on the lower trauma ICU unit where Sarai was walked by. She saw Sarai and thought she knew her. Sarai was resting. The young lady shrugged it off and entered Room B that was next to Sarai's room. The patient in Room B said, "Dee, you came! Hi!"

Dee kissed her sister on the hand and said, "Hi, baby, how are you?" The patient, Keyah, was her younger sister who was healing from her near-death experience. Keyah had been in attendance at an outdoor concert when a disturbed individual started shooting into the crowd. Keyah had undergone a few surgeries to reconstruct her ear that was blown off. She had recently had complications and ended back in the hospital. "Sweetie, I'll be right back," Dee said to Keyah.

"Alright, big sis, I'll be right here," Keyah said smiling. Dee blew her a kiss and went to Room C where Sarai was sleeping. Dee said, "Hello." Sarai opened her eyes. Dee questioned, "Hello, may I pray for you?" Sarai nodded yes. Dee began speaking, "Miss, I pray peace, protection, and healing over you in the name of Jesus. I believe God wants me to tell you not to take any medication because you don't want to hurt the baby you are carrying." Dee touched Sarai's hand. Then she touched Sarai's stomach. Dee spoke in an inaudible voice and left the room.

Sarai opened her eyes in wide disbelief. She wanted to call the young woman back, but she didn't know her name. Sarai was too weak to even open her mouth. Thoughts were racing through her mind, 100 miles per minute. A flood of emotions came rushing in. *GOD? Why would you let this happen? Why would this inconsiderate woman come in here, drop that kind of information, then leave me here to digest it all? How dare she! Who is she, anyway? Can't she see I've been shaken and banged up pretty badly enough?* Sarai began to sweat, feeling nauseous. Her monitors began reading different numbers. This was too much in this moment. After all of these years, she and Adam had been unable to conceive a child, let alone her carry one. She tried to calm herself. Her mind wanted to know. *Where is God? The One who I just gave my life to.* Then, she tried to rationalize. *If I hadn't given my life to Jesus Christ, perhaps all of this wouldn't have happened to me; or if I hadn't given my life to Christ, perhaps I wouldn't be alive.* She looked at her IV and wondered, *Am I on drugs? Is this some kind of test or trick? Where's my husband?* "Jesus help me!" she heard herself say. Sarai went unconscious.

Sarai could hear one of her favorite love songs playing, softly. She was lying in a human-size, woven basket with a snow-white blanket over and under her, cocoon-style. She felt warmth. She felt good—no pain, no worries, and no real thoughts. Peace. Her mother, who had died twelve years ago, came over to the basket, took her hand, and kissed it. She said, "You feel My embrace. This is from your Heavenly Father who loves you so much." Sarai somehow knew it was God talking to her through her mother's being. The voice was that of her mother, but she could feel the power and brilliance that confirmed it could only come from God. Her mother's being continued, "I will always be with you, My daughter. I will never leave or forsake you. My glory will be shown in you and through you. You are Mine, and I am yours. I am your Husband. I am the Bridegroom. All those who seek Me and are chosen are My bride, even your earthly husband, Adam. He will serve Me. You will serve Me well, both in season and out of season. When the time comes, I will return for you. Stay rested in your spirit, My daughter. I am all you both will need." *Selah*.

Her mother's being kissed her forehead. Then she walked away with the angels.

Sarai closed her tear-filled eyes. When she woke up, she could smell the most beautiful fragrance. This encounter was unlike anything she had ever experienced. Adam was stroking her forehead. "Honey?" he said. "Everything is going to be alright."

The nurse was on the other side of the bed. "Mrs. Fulton, how are you feeling?"

Sarai wanted to publicly announce her response. Her thoughts were, *This is the best thing I've ever felt in my life. I've just experienced God on a level most pastors probably have never experienced*. She wanted to tell them that she had just gone to heaven. *I was…*.her thoughts were interrupted…*was I in a basket, or am I a basket case?* She decided not to respond. Sarai wanted to share this whole experience with Delanie Revel before she spoke with anyone else about it. Adam may not believe it.

The nurse continued, "Would you like lunch or anything to drink?" She indicated to Adam where the hospital menu was located on the wall's encasement. Adam ordered two turkey dinners for them both. They both hadn't eaten since lunchtime before the accident, over twenty hours ago.

"I need to eat. Yes, that sounds great!" said Sarai in a raspy voice.

The nurse looked at Adam with concern. "Dr. Fulton, you are going to have to get some rest yourself," she warned. The nurse had reservations about sharing with either of them what the vitals had read minutes ago. The monitor at the nurses station had alerted her that Sarai had flatlined, but when she re-checked them and got to the room, it showed all normal readings. There are times when the computer alerts false alarms, but this was a little extraordinary. The nurse sensed something but could not indicate what. She decided to discuss it with the attending physician. "Are you in any pain, Mrs. Fulton?" asked the nurse.

Sarai shook her head, "No." Sarai turned back to Adam. "Honey, I don't want any pain medication. I don't need any medicine at all. Please don't let them hurt my baby."

"What? Honey, you're tired and probably hungry, yes?" asked Adam.

"I am. You're right. It's been so much."

The nurse was finished checking the IV and monitors. She said, "I'll check on you again, Dr. and Mrs. Fulton. Thank you."

Sarai looked at her loving husband. "Honey, there's a chance I maybe pregnant. Please have them do a pregnancy test. Okay?"

Adam said, "Sure, baby." He did not believe his beautiful wife was in her right mind. He agreed so she wouldn't be upset. "After we eat, I'll look into it. Is that good?"

She nodded feeling a little light-headed but unusually great. Sarai was in no pain.

"Honey, will you contact Mrs. Revel? I need to see her," she asked. The hospital staff worker delivered their lunch.

"Oh my God, Doug! Dr. Sarai is in the hospital. Her and her husband were hit by an F-150!" exclaimed Delanie.

"What?! Are they dead?" replied Doug.

"No! You are so special," said Delanie.

Doug smiled and said, "The way you're shouting, I thought they were killed. What happened?"

Delanie explained, filling Doug in on the details. "She's to be released today."

"Let's pray," they both decided simultaneously. When they finished, Delanie asked Doug if he would join her and Dionne tomorrow when they went to visit the Fultons.

Doug said, "I'll reschedule my meeting with my sound man." Doug was a producer at Channel 4 TV station. He was at the top of his career, winning an Emmy for his piece on absent fathers. He needed a day off.

Dionne overheard them. "Mom, can I bring my Hello Kitty scrapbook?" Dionne had been working on her latest project all summer. She planned to bring it to the creative arts class in the fall when school started.

"Oh, my baby has been doing a great job, Doug." said Delanie. "You sure can, my big girl."

"Yay! Thank you, Mommy. Thank you, Daddy." Dionne was grateful. The next day as they were headed to the Drs. Adam and Sarai Fulton's home, the twins pulled up.

"What car are we taking, Doug?" asked Delanie.

He replied, "Let's take the Audi."

"Hey, Dad. Hey, Mom," said the twins. They usually spoke in unison.

"Hi, boys," said Dionne with her scrapbook under her arm.

Her older brothers playfully roughed her up. "Who you calling boy, girl?" said Treyvon.

"Stop!" said Doug. "Don't mess with my princess. Right, babe?" he said, winking at Delanie.

"That's right. Don't make me use my black belt crush on you two." Delanie was hugging them both by this time. Doug greeted their sons with hand clasps and a shoulder clutch for each one.

Doug smiled, "Good to see y'all, man. We don't have any food, either."

"We ate, already," said Trevor with a smirk on his face. "Where you going?"

Doug replied, " We are going to Dr. Fulton's home. They were in a car accident. We are visiting. You met the wife, Dr. Sarai, when we had that family session months ago."

"Aw-w-w man, is she alright?" said Treyvon.

"Yes...or she will be. Want to join us?" asked Doug.

"What time you think we'll be back here?" asked Trevor.

"About an hour, or so," said Delanie.

"Okay." the twins agreed to go, too. *Good idea they were driving the Audi SUV so that everyone could fit comfortably*, Doug thought to himself. They arrived at the Fultons' home before rush hour. They collectively prayed before getting out of the vehicle. Delanie and Doug both agreed it was necessary to cover their children and all that was dear to them on these assignments or visits.

We are all assigned, on this earth, to serve and worship God, then serve and love on others. That is our reasonable response to a Savior, a loving Father, who art in Heaven, whose name is above all names. Thank God for wisdom and understanding on these matters. In order for them to serve the Lord God in delivering and winning souls to Jesus Christ and His kingdom, it was required to be equipped in spiritual warfare that begins and ends with prayer. Use of the Word of God is key. It requires those who are helping set the captives free to use God's Word and, most importantly, the name of Jesus.

Adam met them in their mile-long driveway that led to a large massive, colonial home. It had columns and was surrounded by willow trees. The landscaping was precise.

"Wow!" said the young people in the Audi as they drove up. The land had to be no less than eighteen acres. The backdrop was the mountains.

"Hello, hello," said Doug as he and Dr. Adam shook hands. Doug introduced his family to Dr. Adam Fulton. Dr. Sarai managed to walk, slowly, out on one of the patios escorted by a private nurse. The twins and Dionne grabbed their takeout, which had been picked up on the way. The Revels didn't want to impose on the Fultons to provide a meal for them, especially given the occasion. Delanie had called ahead to notify the Fultons that she was bringing her family of five. Dr. Sarai gave the okay and was delighted they all were coming.

Delanie hid her deep concern. She couldn't dispel the uneasy feeling in her spirit. She did not know what it was, but it was something big, one of those pivotal moments that was going to touch and change lives drastically. She had recognized it in the past. Then, she wasn't as spiritually trained as she was now. Every now and then, Doug would hug Delanie or clasp her hands in his. He may have been sensing it or just knew something was troubling his wife.

"Hi, Dr. Sarai," said Delanie as she smiled.

"Hello Delanie and Douglas. Wow, look at how the children have grown!" exclaimed Dr. Sarai.

"When you hug, please be gentle," warned the private nurse as everyone embraced one another.

"Come in. Malaina Mallory, our housekeeper, will show you the way to the kitchen so you can get something cold to drink, and you young people can get settled on the backyard patio to eat your takeout. There's a game room entrance on that side of the house, also," said Adam. He continued, "My wife may need to retire to the family room to recline and put her feet up. Okay, babe?"

"Yes, dear," said Dr. Sarai jokingly, in a robotic sounding voice. The adults laughed. Treyvon, Trevor, and Dionne were headed toward the game room. Dionne had to run to the SUV and get her scrapbook.

"Eat first, guys!" shouted Delanie.

"Do you shoot pool?" Adam asked Doug. "Come on, Doug, shall we join the children and get a quick pool game in?"

Now Doug was excited. "I put the p-o in pool, man."

"Aw-w-w…" everyone said simultaneously.

The women headed inside the house. "You look great, Dr. Sarai," said Delanie.

"I feel surprisingly great. It must be the hand of God. He has me covered," she replied.

"I can see that," agreed Delanie.

"I can give you a short tour of the house while I tell you about my last few days, Delanie. It has been unbelievable," said Dr. Sarai.

"I'll have to charge you by the half hour, counselor," said Delanie. They both laughed. Let's begin in prayer:

Daddy God,

There truly is none like you. You're excellent in all your ways. You are the one and only true God. Your daughters are coming before you in humility and love. We are acknowledging your Son, Jesus, for all of His love and sacrifice. Dr. Sarai has just experienced you on a level that many will not experience in their years on earth. You have chosen her, just like Sarah in biblical times, to be a miracle and a mother of a miracle. She was barren, but you, God, have blessed her and her husband. No longer will they feel the emptiness in this area. She repents for not knowing or seeking you in the past. Oh, but how merciful and gracious you are to us all. Thank you for peace, protection, and provision. Thank you for this healthy child that the Fultons will deliver in seven months. This is evidence of Your glory—a life given to Dr. Sarai and Dr. Adam for them to dedicate this beautiful child back to You in faith and love. Thank you for being the author and finisher of our faith. Thank you for a victorious destiny. Dr. Adam and Dr. Sarai will worship You in spirit and in truth. Thank you for finding the right church and strategic, Godly support in developing them. Most importantly, thank you for be The Counselor who truly heals all wounds, words, and sins. This couple will overcome all obstacles and the adversary. Your ways and Your will be done. We love you, Lord. In Jesus's' matchless name, Amen.

"Amen," said Dr. Sarai. "So you know. That confirms that—it's absolutely unbelievable. I'm so grateful. I'm grateful I met you, Delanie. I'm grateful to God. At first, I thought God had failed me. I know I'm new to this relationship choosing to serve God. But He really moves fast. Don't He know my world is shifting. This is really exciting, scary, adventurous, exhausting, glorifying, amazing. One moment, I'm comfortable in my practice with all the checks and balances. My husband and I were cozy in our practices, having the answers to others' problems. Now I'm speaking in fragmented sentences, searching for the words to use."

Delanie thought, *Just wait until you start researching His Word.*

Dr. Sarai said, "And am I making sense?"

Delanie smiled and rolled her eyes around. "Yes, ma'am." Dr. Sarai then threw a balled-up tissue at her. *Oh, Dr. Fulton is loosening up! Where's the ole "type-A," got-it-all together personality?*

Dr. Sarai continued, "What am I to do with a baby with our practices in full bloom? Will Adam make a good father? Is this really what he wants at this time?"

She was anxious for them to talk. "I have so many questions. I believe Adam is accepting my new relationship with God. I believe he will accept Jesus as his Lord and Savior. I hope it's soon. I've been watching YouTube sermons. We must be equally yoked, yes?" She didn't let Delanie respond before her next comment. *Wow! Look who's talking now,* thought Delanie.

"How will we raise our child…" Dr. Sarai didn't finish her question.

Delanie began to sing the most beautiful song that Dr. Sarai had heard in many years. "Be not dismayed. Whatever you ask, God will take care of you," sang Delanie.

Peace flooded the atmosphere in the room.

Doug and Dr. Adam were loud and competitive. Doug was winning the third game of pool. "Ah-h-h," said Doug as the 8-ball dropped in the corner pocket.

"Good game," relinquished Dr. Adam. The twins high-fived one another. Then they high fived their dad. Dionne was looking through her scrapbook, rearranging her photos again.

Dr. Adam approached Doug. "We will have to invite you to our club's event in the Colorado mountains. I could use a partner to whip up on some of my colleagues in the annual tournament in between our conference schedule. You and your wife would love it. Sarai and I have been attending for years. She…" he stopped abruptly. "She may or may not be able to go." He had forgotten she was pregnant. He found it hard to believe they conceived a child. Thoughts rushed in, and his facial expression changed.

"You alright, man?" asked Doug.

"Yeah, yes, I'm good…just remembering something," Adam said. He wasn't sure he should share their recent surprise, yet.

Doug's sensors went on high alert. He had the gift of discernment. "Lord, please reveal what it is," he silently prayed. Doug made a shivering gesture saying, "Colorado is cold, man. But the wife and I would like to take you up on the invite."

Dr. Adam responded, "It's in February. I'll have my secretary email you the information with the itinerary and room assignments. It's in Helen, Colorado."

"Helen, Colorado?" said the twins simultaneously.

Why does that sound familiar? Doug thought. A few of Dionne's pictures fell out of her scrapbook. Everyone was distracted for a minute or two. Dr. Adam and the twins reached to retrieve them. The twins picked up the pictures of themselves when they were four years old, along with pictures of Doug and Delanie's wedding. Dr. Adam picked up the one with Nina holding her two newborns. They were about seven months old.

As he looked at the picture, he said, "Here you go, little lady," to Dionne. When he handed the photo to Dionne, he became aware of what he saw. His mouth opened. Dr. Adam dropped the picture. His face turned white in disbelief. He gathered himself when he realized everyone was watching his behavior. He said, "Excuse me…so clumsy."

The twins looked amazed. Treyvon said, "That's us." He said, playfully, "We look that bad, Dr. Adam? That's our biological mother holding us when we were seven months old."

Trevor then said, "We don't remember her all that good."

Doug corrected him. "All that well."

Dionne said, "Thank you." She looked in Dr. Adam's direction. "You, alright? You look like you saw a ghost—spooked and everything."

"Yes, little lady. I'm fine," was Dr. Adam's response.

Doug chimed in, "We all know that fine is an acronym for 'fanatically insane, narcissistically erratic.' Yes sir, Doctor. Do you know her by some chance? Her name was Nina."

"No," replied Dr. Adam, shaking his head. The color in his face returned, slightly.

Doug immediately knew he was lying. He suddenly remembered Nina had been heading up to the mountains in Helen, Colorado, when she died.

For there is nothing hidden that will not be disclosed, and nothing concealed that will not be made known and brought to light.
Luke 8:17 (NIV), Matthew 10:26, Mark 4:22 (NKJV)

"Well, we'd better check on our wives," said Dr. Adam. He led everyone through his massive house, giving them a brief tour along the way. His persona had totally changed. When they reached Delanie and Dr. Sarai, the two women were in tears—tears of laughter, tears of joy.

Dr. Sarai had shared with Delanie all about her encounter with God at the hospital. Delanie had helped her interpret the vision. *It is a relief and a blessing to get some understanding,* thought Dr. Sarai. She was grateful for her new mentor. Who would have imagined things would happen this way? Who would have thought this would be the path all of their lives would be traveling? That's the kind of God we serve.

The Revels said their goodbyes and agreed to connect again soon. The twins had a great time. They had forgotten they were to meet some friends to help them move. When they arrived home, they hugged their parents, roughed up Dionne, and promised to come over for dinner and family game night. They jumped into their car to pull off, but not before Doug went to their car, looked at them closely, and turned the volume on their music system down.

"Be safe, man. May God bless you both."

Delanie picked up on the gesture. "Why did you do that, babe?"

Doug winked at her. "I got something for you later."

Oh, yeah, she thought.

After the day was coming to a close, Dionne was in her messy but, beautifully decorated room saying her prayers. Delanie slid into her sexy homemade lingerie. Victoria's Secret had nothing on this wear. Delanie was a very creative woman. She had designed this Spandex body shaper dress with detachable straps. She had creatively cut holes where her "girls" could be exposed. She had curved slits through the one piece. It was provocative and sort of risqué. She placed her silky body cream in places where "the sun don't shine" and all over. *Anoint yourself with oil.* She pictured her beautiful husband and how she would put oil on him as she waited on the chaise lounge in their bedroom.

God has created intimacy between a husband and a wife, only in marriage, that is ordained by Him. He anoints us with an oil, too. It's an oil of sealant, confirming we are His. It's an oil of gladness.

Now it is God who makes both us and you stand firm in Christ. He anointed us, set his seal of ownership on us, and put His Spirit In our hearts as a deposit, guaranteeing what is to come.
2 Corinthians 1:21-22. (NIV)

You have loved righteousness and hated wickedness. Therefore, God, your God, has anointed you with the oil of gladness beyond your companions.
Psalm 45:7(NIV)

Doug came upstairs from locking and shutting everything off throughout the house. He could smell her before he saw her. Nice! "Aw-w-w, babe! You look so sexy and smell so sweet. Babe, as much as I want to go where you want to take me, I have to talk to you. It can't wait." Doug was focused.

If Delanie could cuss, she would have right then. Now, he wants to talk. What's going on? Usually, she was the one who did the talking. First, it was Dr. Sarai with a lot on her mind. Now, Doug of all people? She regrouped. If Doug wanted to talk in lieu of jumping her bones, it must be important. Wait…if he wants to talk, period, it must be very important. "I'm all ears, babe," she said as she stretched her legs around his waist when he settled near her.

"I'm going out on a ledge here, but I have a gut feeling that ole Dr. Fulton has major skeletons in the closet." Doug went on. "He and his colleagues get together annually in Helen, Colorado…"

Delanie stopped him, "Babe, this requires prayer and covering." She anointed both their heads then, flirtatiously, and rubbed some on his neck and bare shoulders.

Doug led the prayer, speaking in his language. When the prayer was lifted, he continued. "Dr. Fulton and his colleagues hold an annual conference. In between their sessions, they hold a pool tournament. He's feeling my game," he said, playfully. "He has invited us to join them and have me as his partner in the tournament. It's some time in February."

"Dr. Sarai is pregnant, Doug," said Delanie. "Does he know his wife may be delivering around said time?"

"Oh-h-h, that's why he was acting secretive at first when he extended the invite. But, it really got different when Dionne dropped pictures from her scrapbook. They were pictures of Nina and the twins. Dear ole Dr. Fulton looked at Nina, and you would have thought the blood left his body—ghost-like stuff, babe." Doug continued, filling Delanie with the specifics of what everyone said, how Dr. Adam's demeanor changed, and how their tour went. Delanie was very attentive. "I think he knew Nina. And knowing Nina, they probably were sleeping together. Babe, I looked at our beautiful sons before they left tonight, and I see a resemblance to the good ole doctor," Doug finished commenting.

Delanie knew something felt uneasy before they'd arrived to the Fultons' home.

"Babe, let's not jump to any conclusions. I have to admit, I'm feeling you on this one."

"Adam, I'm so thrilled about us finally having a child. I'm so glad that accident didn't harm our baby. God protected me, too. Wouldn't you say?" Sarai said, waiting for a response. Adam was in the bathroom. "What are you doing? Come rub my feet, please. I'll rub your back, you rub mine…"

Adam had been beside himself ever since he saw the picture of his beloved Nina. He had put her, completely, out of his mind for years. His heart began to hurt and long for her. He thought his secret affair had died with her. He buried the feelings of guilt and betrayal to Sarai. Sarai—always the beautiful, wonderful wife. But his insatiable desire for Nina had trumped that. Sin always entertains us. Lust always tricks and traps us into believing the complete opposite of what God desires for us, tells us, and shows us. It's the age-old agenda to destroy God's plan and our destiny. With all the knowledge and information at our fingertips, one would think more of us would be able to overcome the ignorance that leads to sin. We can construct the state of the art this or that but can't seem to master self-control, humility, and the following of our beautiful, and gracious God.

Lord, help us!

If My People who are called, by My Name, will humble themselves, and pray. Seek My Face, turn from their wicked ways, then I will hear from heaven and I will forgive their sins and heal their land.
2 Chronicles 7:14 NKJV

"Alright, dearest lady, I'll be right there," said Adam. He was thinking, *After I get right*. He tossed his head back and swallowed little white pills, then chased them with water. "Here, I come." He ran into their bedroom, stopped, and gently scooped his clueless wife up. He had made a conscious effort to stop self-medicating himself with the sample meds that his office so regularly received. He had been doing good. Now, this—his wife being led into religion, the car accident, their finances being slightly affected because she was home recuperating, his carrying the responsibility of both practices, the investigation of the man who had hit them, handling the repairs through their insurances, a new baby, and the possibility that Sarai would find out he had been cheating on her during their engagement. Well, at least they hadn't been married yet. He thought. That's where Adam was wrong.

Throughout Scripture, God confirms He is all-knowing. He is detailed. He has a plan for each and every one of us, especially, when it comes to marriage. He knows and has designed each one to be with, live with, and/or do life with the other.

Nevertheless. Because of sexual immorality, let each man have his own wife, and let each woman have her own husband.
I Corinthians 7:2 NKJV

God will divinely connect you to your spouse (whether one will attest to this truth or not).

---

*He that finds a wife finds a good thing and obtains favor
from the Lord.
Proverbs 18:22*

That's exactly it. The male/man is to find the wife God has chosen for him. He is to choose to get guidance from his biological father or the man who stands in proxy for him (if the father is deceased) in making his choice as unto God. The males, together, should seek the guidance and the power of God, the Holy Spirit. The decision is not based on looks, material things, assets, and especially not emotions. All of us are required to model godliness seeking direction from God, always. God is always there. Even when our natural father is not. Ask Him, "Show me, Lord, who is to be my spouse." When the spouse is found, make it a covenant to love and cherish her 'til death due you part. It will bring harmony to many.

The world culture as it is today isn't much of a society. *Society- an organized group of persons associated together for religious, benevolent, cultural, scientific, political, patriarch, or other persons. (dictionary.com, n.d.)*

Society- A body of individuals living as members of a community sharing traditions, laws, and values.

Society- a voluntary association of individuals for common ends especially an organized group working together or periodically meeting because of common interest, beliefs, professions 2. a community, nation or broad grouping of people having common tradtions, institutions, and collective activities and interests.

(Merian-Webster, n.d . accessed 2020)

It barely resembles a civilization. People are choosing to be as corrupt and self-indulging, just as the Bible shows us in the books of Genesis, Judges, Kings, and Revelation. There will not be world peace until Jesus returns. We can rely on this truth.

God's original plan for us is marriage, multiplication, reverence, and the worshipping of Him. He requires us to love and have godly relationships. Man has flipped the script. Humans have deviated from godliness and have selfishly sunk into sin.

"I hate divorce," says the Lord.
Malachi 2:16 NIV "

For the Lord God of Israel says that He hates divorce. For it covers one's garment with violence, "says The Lord of Hosts. "Therefore take heed to your spirit. That you do not deal treacherously."

God hates it because it can be so destructive. The Antichrist loves it. It is a result of sin.

Most of those who chose divorce, instead of fighting for unity between themselves, operate in pride. They are fighting a losing battle unless both are willing or are able to humble themselves. Elect to be grateful for what God has given you. Gratitude for one another causes one to operate in the mindset of success. It creates a closer relationship to God.

The spirit of divorce not only destroys families. Most importantly, it destroys our relationship with God. It brings hardship in churches, communities, and nations. One divorce usually leads to more divorces—more separation from God. But thank God for Jesus! His sacrificial blood has given us grace. And that amazing Triune God has a way of turning what is meant for evil around for our good.

But as for you, ye thought evil against me; but, God meant it unto good, to bring to pass, as it is this day, to save much people alive.
Gen 50:20 KJV

When a spouse divorces you without your consent, it will, ultimately and in due season, cause the injured spouse to be closer to God. The spouse is now married to God without the responsibility to submit to a spouse. The pain divorce causes can drive you right into the arms of the Father.

If one can honor marriage, one will be very equipped to be with our Father, Lord God, forever in eternity. Staying married causes you to, most likely, have increased faith, humility, a sacrificial nature, and patience. Simply said, marriage is the trial run of the relationship we are to have with God. It will bring forth the fruit of the Spirit of God. In other words, you will adopt the character of God when you love unconditionally, forgive freely (because you have a lot to be forgiven for), have patience more so than not, show kindness, possess goodness, have humility that supersedes pride, and are willing to sacrifice often, which is to "suffer for Me," says the Lord.

Would Dr. Sarai be willing to suffer for Jesus? She had now given herself and accepted Jesus's offer to be her personal Savior. Would she embrace God's love when she discovered the hidden secrets her husband had held for so long? The divine order of things will bring the truth out every time.

This was one time that Delanie was deeply unwilling to be the one to tell Dr. Sarai about her husband Adam. Dr. Sarai was reading everything relating to motherhood. She was also reading the Bible while challenging anything or anyone who believed God was not God. You could not tell her God was not a good God and seated in high places. She felt compelled to share how He had secured her from losing her miracle baby boy. Now in her second trimester, she and Adam had learned the sex of their baby. Adam was excited and scared. He was exhausted, too. The secret was wearing on him but, he would not share his secrets for fear of destroying their family or, worse, cause his beautiful wife to miscarry.

Adam was beginning to seek God more often. He believed he had no one to go to. He couldn't share his feelings with his wife. He refused to let his colleagues know. His family would probably post it on Facebook or YouTube. Adam cried out to God one night after he almost overdosed. He was home alone. Sarai had gone away with Delanie and a couple of other friends to a retreat. He took some Vicodins and threw some salmon steaks on the grill. He thought he heard Nina's voice. It was, in actuality, a movie on Showtime instead. Adam called Doug to see if he wanted to shoot pool since their wives were away. Doug answered. After the call ended, Doug heard God's voice: "My son, it is time." Doug heard it clearly in an audible voice.

Doug found a sitter for Dionne and arrived a couple of hours later to Adam's house to find Adam on the floor in his foyer. Blood was coming from Adam's mouth. He didn't seem to have fallen down the stairs or hit anything. His pulse was faint. Adam apparently had been coming in or going out of the door because the door was unlocked. Where were the housekeepers? Doug immediately shouted, "God, we need You, Jesus!"

Adam opened his eyes them shut them. Doug called 9-1-1 and began CPR. Adam came to. He said, "Damn, what have you been eating?" Doug put his hand over his own mouth to check his own breath. The onions on his tuna sub were evident.

He smirked, "Shut up, man, and get off this floor by yourself."

The EMTs arrived. Adam was checked. He wanted to avoid going to the hospital for fear that his latest secret addiction would be discovered. He let the EMTs know his credentials as a doctor and that he would do follow-up procedures at his office on Monday. Doug called his cousin Shaina to let her know that he would pick Dionne up in the morning. It was going to be a long night.

Doug was prepared to do battle with Adam's strongholds, to his lack of surrender to the living God, to his addictions. Doug was shown in his spirit that God was ready for Adam to answer the call on his life. Doug called his male fellowship group. He gave them Adam's address after asking Adam if a few of his buddies could join them since the salmon steaks were nice and grilled. He didn't mention the warfare that was about to take place.

Dr. Adam was light-headed and mostly confused. He was in no shape to play pool or argue. He thought he heard a faint voice. Did he hear God or was it the pills? He tried to reason within his thoughts. The three men arrived. Doug was given permission to open the door to welcome them. "Hey, man, how are you guys doing?" Doug shook hands and bumped shoulders.

"Wow! Who lives here, a celebrity?" said one guy.

Doug whispered to the group of men. "One of God's elect who needs to surrender and be delivered—set free." They piled hands while in a circle. They began to pray in the spirit, and the deliverance commenced. They convened in the sitting area near the patio where Adam moved to and was seated. Doug introduced his group to Adam.

Adam said, "I know what you're here for," in a deep deceptive voice that was not his. The enemy had manifested in Adam.

"We call forth Adam," said the group simultaneously. One of the men sang very loudly in a baritone voice. One man prayed loudly in the spirit. The third man called out the evil spirits one by one, mentioning Jesus's name all throughout. Doug recited scriptures Psalm 91, Judges 6:24-34, Deuteronomy 5:9-10, Galatians 3:13-14, Isaiah 54:17, Joel 2:27-28, Matthew 16:18-19, Joel 2:23-27, and Luke 10:18-19. The deliverance went on for an hour. Then complete silence.

Adam's phone mysteriously went on mute. God was not going to permit any distractions. It was Sarai. She wanted to tell her husband she loved him. Delanie was praying at that very moment because she could sense her husband needed her to pray warfare over those 400 miles away.

"Thank you, Jesus," the men said when it was done. Adam was stretched out on the floor. He was slain in the Spirit. He could not get up until he was released. He cried aloud. He rolled over.

He said, "Jesus, I surrender to You! I'm so sorry for all that I've done. I'm Yours, God." There was a strong odor emitting in the atmosphere. The men placed oil on their hands. They touched Adam's forehead, chest near his heart, arms, and legs. Silence again.

Then Adam defecated and said he had to go to the bathroom, despite the fact that he had already gone on himself.

Adam was asked, "Do you accept Jesus Christ into your life, confessing He is Lord, believing that in your heart, and choosing to follow Him all the days of your life?"

"Yes, Yes!" cried Adam. "I'm so sorry, God." They helped him up just in time to get him to the kitchen sink. Adam vomited and cried. He cried out, "Jesus loves me!"

The deliverance was complete. The process to follow God's plan on this level for his life had been set in motion. Adam's destiny as a child of the King was brought into fruition.

"Okay, man, let's get you cleaned up," said one of the men.

As I live, says The Lord, every knee shall bow to Me, and every tongue shall confess to God.
Romans 14:11 NKJV

The men left around 5:00 am in the morning. Doug stayed with Adam until Sarai returned that afternoon.

Adam was a new man in Christ—born again, sin forgiven, a representative of the kingdom of the Most High. His wife returned home to a new man. She kept asking him questions because she saw a difference in him. He wanted her to tell him more about Jesus than ever before. Adam decided to tell Sarai everything about Nina after the delivery of their baby. He spent the next three months cherishing the love they had. He did not think about Nina anymore. The drug addiction ended the night he was delivered with the help of those faithful men of God. Adam began to spend time with these men who stood on the front line for his soul, while being groomed in the things of the

Father. Dr. Adam was prepared when Sarai delivered a healthy baby boy on Thanksgiving Day, a day of harvest— 6 pounds, 11 ounces was what this miracle baby weighed. They dedicated their child to God in the subsequent months.

On the day of the dedication, Doug and Delanie received some not-so-celebratory news of their own. The resemblance of their strong, handsome sons, Trevor and Treyvon, to Dr. Adam was becoming more pronounced. They had their sons tested for paternity months prior. They told their sons it was for a possible organ donation in case one of them needed it. That was only partially true. Doug and Delanie were joined by their pastors when the results were opened. They felt they would need their guidance in this situation. The results showed there was zero percentage that Trevor and Treyvon could be Doug's sons. Delanie's tears could not stop. Doug wailed. The pastors' eyes filled because the atmosphere was so painful. Everyone hugged Doug. This wonderful man had raised those boys with the love of the Father. He was an anointed husband, father, and role model for his entire family. Delanie was right by his side, helping and making it easier for him to do so. Now, this.

Delanie suddenly came to the most profound conclusion. "God will heal us, babe. God chose us to impart and implant His love, spirit, and principles in our sons, Doug. We were chosen, not Nina nor Adam. It was us. You will continue to be their father and I, their mother. No one will take that away." Just as she finished, the twins busted in the house, playfully, hitting one another with a foam decal from the championship game at their college. One twin fell down and slid right next to where his Dad was kneeling.

"Hey, Dad, what up?" Treyvon said. Doug gathered himself. God came through once again. Doug grabbed him and hugged him.

"Get over here," Doug said to his other son. They huddled. Delanie joined in. The pastors rubbed their backs.

The time was not given to Doug and Delanie of when this revelation was to be shared. Testing for Adam and the twins would have to be arranged. But they knew one day God would orchestrate it, and it would be right on time. They trusted Him.

Evaluation of the Characters under the Influence of Evil Spirits

The spirt of:

Pride–the original, most serious of all sins and the ultimate source from which others arise. It is the desire to be more important or attractive than others, failure to acknowledge the good works of others, and excessive love of self (especially holding self out of proper position toward God). It is related to vanity. Belief in one's own abilities or attractiveness. The quality or state of being proud, inordinate self-esteem.

The spirit of deception- the enemy had deceived each one of their true identity, their purpose, God's plan, and their destiny. None of them were equipped with a solid relationship with Jesus Christ. This derails most people at birth—the not knowing of oneself or their purpose in life by operating in spiritual blindness. Accepting the lies of the enemy and workers of iniquity.

The spirit of rebellion- refusal to live according to God's principles, values, and guidance. Sin comes in like a flood, making a more ordered life more difficult and complicated. This in not God's plan. Sin leads to death.

The spirit of lust- It's all about me. It's about what I want. Thoughts of excessive sex. Overly consumed with things or people. Too intense desire or need. Greed.

Matthew 5:28

Lying spirit- one lie leads to another, leads to strongholds, addictions, and curses. Only the truth will set people free. Hypocrisy and deception.

Covetous spirit- marked by inordinate desire for wealth or possession belonging to other people (including spouses, children, etc.).

Proverbs 16:18

Envy–painful or resentful awareness of an advantage enjoyed by another, joined with a desire to possess the same advantage. Like greed. Resentment that another person has something they perceive themselves as lacking, and they wish the person to be deprived of it.

I Peter 2:1-2

Jealousy–the thoughts or feelings of insecurity, fear, and concern over lack of possessions, talents, abilities, relationships. Feelings of inadequacy, disgust, or helplessness. Carnal-minded people who envy others of who they are or possess. It produces strife and division.

Spirit of Infirmity–specific evil spirits that cause physical maladies. Jesus specifically speaks of Satan having bound a woman (Luke 13:16). Many human ailments are caused by living in a sinful world.

Ephesians 6:12, Luke 13

Spirit of strife–a quarrelsome spirit that sows evil and lack of clarity. It creates an angry undercurrent or an unhealthy environment. Consistent bickering and disagreement.

Spirit of Pharmacia–the use of mind-altering drugs, both legal and illegal. This spirit is associated with medicine, spells, poisoning, and witchcraft. Pharmacia's Greek translation is "witchcraft." (Wilkepedia, n. d. accessed 2020) captive to sin by way of addiction to medicine.

Galatians 5:19-21, Revelation 9:21, 18:23

Anger–the root cause of this spirit is unforgiveness. The holding on of tensions from past hurts and guilt. A person who is dealing with unresolved emotional dysfunctional behavior.

Murder/Suicide–a wicked spirit of madness and recklessness. The attitude of murder starts in the heart and mind. Brooding anger, contempt, and character assassination. Selfish anger that leads to the killing of someone or self.

The occult/sadism–the belief in and/or invocation and worship of Satan. An occult sadist seals pacts with dark spirits. Those involved practice witchcraft, calling spirits, astrology, fortune telling, false religions, etc.

False religions–teachings and practices that come to you in the name of Jesus but do not teach the truth. It's the preaching of a counterfeit gospel and/or one that has great deception.

Different vices–negative characteristics associated with transgressions. Antagonism, anger, and arrogance are some of the temperament/traits. Virtue is not present or evident.

Revenge–retribution or repayment from those harmed. To avenge, making someone accountable for his or her infractions. Action taken by an unforgiving soul.

Hatred–developed as a result of a poisoned heart rooted in bitterness and anger. Suicide, murder, and fear are a result of this spirit.

Adultery–the marriage bed that is defiled by immorality and other sexual sins. Those who have illegal sex acts. Christians who finds pleasure in the things that Satan offers.

Fornication–sexual intercourse between people who are not married to each other. Also, refers to any violation of God's laws regarding sexual behavior. Demon of lust and perversion.

Extravagance–unrestrained excess, indulgence in sensual pleasures, involving sex, alcohol, or drugs.

Greed- excessive or reprehensible acquisitiveness. Like gluttony. A sin of excess. Very rapacious desire and pursuit of wealth. Theft, robbery, especially by means of trickery or manipulation.

Ephesians 4:19

Acedia- neglect to take care of something that one should. Suppression of emotions as concerns, excitement, motivation, and passion. Insensible or uncaring.

Depression/despair–feelings of hopelessness, impending doom.

Sloth–failure to use one's talents and gifts. Viewed as laziness and indifference.

Wrath- strong, vengeful anger or indignation. Known as anger or rage, uncontrolled or inordinate feelings of hatred and anger, which can manifest into impatience, revenge, and vigilantism. Suicide is deemed as the ultimate, albeit tragic, expression or wrath.

Proverbs 15:1

Vainglory–unjustified boasting

Laziness–disinclined to activity or exertion, not energetic or vigorous.

Proverbs 15:19

Apathy- not interest in things generally considered interesting or moving. Absence of passion, emotions, or excitement. Spiritless.

Psychological manipulation- influence to change behavior of others through deception or abusive behavior by advancing only the interest of the manipulator.

Narcissism- refers to the trait egotism. The spirit that causes one to believe they are the most skilled, competent, and best-looking—living with a twisted sense of superiority and perfection. Lack of empathy. Selfish, needing constant attention.

Fear–an unpleasant emotion caused by the belief that someone or something is dangerous, likely to cause pain or a threat. To be afraid of someone or something harmful. Loss of courage.

2 Timothy 1:7

Worry–to be burdened. It is derived from Anglo-Saxon word meaning "to choke" or "to strangle." It is a form of fear or uncertainty that causes one to focus on the problem. Worry controls and causes one to waste emotional and spiritual energy. It leads to depression and Gluttony- excess eating and drinking. Overindulgence or overconsumption of anything to the point of waste.

Proverbs 23:21

Logorrhea spirit–pathologically excessive and often incoherent talkativeness or wordiness that is a characteristic especially of manic phase of bi-polar disorder. Repetitive speech. Compulsive rhetoric.

Jezebel spirit–this is one of the nastiest, evil, most disgusting, cunning, and seductive spirit in Satan's hierarchy. The Queen

Jezebel was in authority, leading others into idol worship and murder. She was responsible for the killing of many prophets. It is a very controlling spirit. Some personality traits to identify them are (but not limited to) evil, hateful, cold, ruthless, liars, cheaters, highly self-centered/narcissistic, judgmental, critical, condescending, demanding, giving false prophecies, highly lustful, hating prophets/prayer, combative/confrontational, maximum pride.

Matthew 22:37, Acts 24:14,

Spirit of inertia–reluctant to cooperate with changes in your motion and acceleration when one is on the wrong path, causing force to be exerted on oneself that makes him or her move differently when he or she doesn't want or intend to. Willingness to stay in sin until something forces him or her to choose otherwise.

Familiar spirit–It manipulates people with false prophecy, false dreams, and vision.

Charmers, mediums, divination, soothsaying, interpretation of omens, and sorcery are under the influence and control of this spirit.

Marine spirits- This class of demons are responsible for all the whoredom our world is living with today. They perpetrate the highest level of wickedness against mankind in the form of filth, defilements, sexual bondages, depravity, marital breakups, and disillusionments. They operate through water.

Strong Man spirit–ruler of darkness that controls governments, laws, and thoughts of people or nations. Represents persons in authority such as kings, leaders, generals, etc., who take dominion and power corruptively.

The Bible tells us in Matthew 12:43 there are levels of wickedness in Satan's kingdom. The Bible tell us truths that are even more powerful.

*Then I saw a great white throne and Him who sat on it, from whose face the earth and the heaven fled away. And there was found no place for them. And I saw the dead, small and great, standing before God, and the books were opened. And another book was opened, which is the Book of Life. And the dead were judged according to their works, by the things which were written in the books. The sea gave up the dead who were in it, and Death and Hades delivered up the dead who were in them. And they were judged, each one according to his works. Then Death and Hades were cast into the lake of fire. This is the second death. And anyone **not** found written in the Book of Life was cast into the lake of fire.*

Revelation 20:11-15.

Please get off Facebook and put your face in The Book— The Bible.

The strategy in the war against evil spiritual warfare is (but not limited to):

Recognize, repent, read God's Word, relentlessly pray and fast, reconcile to the things of God and His kingdom, relax

and trust God, resist demonic influences, release evil ties and worldliness, receive the transformation, receive the relationship with God via the Holy Spirit, redemption is yours. Now walk in your freedom with Jesus Christ with a purely, renewed heart.

Selah.

CPSIA information can be obtained
at www.ICGtesting.com
Printed in the USA
LVHW010915310720
661938LV00008B/661

9 781631 293993